THE ■ CHINESE ■ KIT
ASTROLOGY

Book of
Interpretations

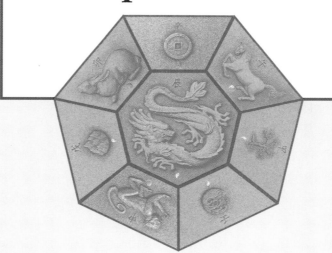

THE CHINESE ASTROLOGY KIT

Book of Interpretations

DEREK WALTERS AND HELEN JONES

JOURNEY EDITIONS
BOSTON • TOKYO • SINGAPORE

Dedicated with respectful gratitude to my dear friend and honoured teacher,
Grandmaster Richard Tsui, Soothsayer, The Temple of Wong Tai Sin

First published in the United States in 2001 by Journey Editions,
an imprint of Periplus Editions (HK) Ltd., with editorial offices at
153 Milk Street, Boston, Massachusetts 02109.

ISBN: 1-58290-060-4

Distributed by

NORTH AMERICA
Tuttle Publishing
Distribution Center
Airport Industrial Park
364 Innovation Drive
North Clarendon,
VT 05759-9436
Tel: (802) 773-8930
Tel: (800) 526-2778
Fax: (802) 773-6993

JAPAN
Tuttle Publishing
RK Building, 2nd Floor
2-13-10 Shimo-Meguro,
Meguro-Ku
Tokyo 153 0064
Tel: (03) 5437-0171
Fax: (03) 5437-0755

SOUTHEAST ASIA
Berkeley Books Pte Ltd
5 Little Road #08-01
Singapore 536983
Tel: (65) 280-1330
Fax: (65) 280-6290

First edition
07 06 05 04 03 02 01   10 9 8 7 6 5 4 3 2 1

AN EDDISON • SADD EDITION
Edited, designed and produced by
Eddison Sadd Editions Limited
St Chad's House, 148 King's Cross Road
London WC1X 9DH

Phototypeset in New Baskerville BT and Frutiger
using QuarkXPress on Apple Macintosh.
Origination by Bright Arts, Singapore.
Printed and bound by Hung Hing Offset
Printing Co. Ltd., China.

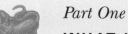
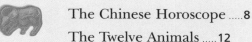
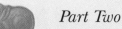

C
O
N
T
E
N
T
S

甚麼是命數

Part One

WHAT IS CHINESE ASTROLOGY?

During holiday time in Hong Kong, Taiwan and, nowadays, even mainland China itself, the temples throng with people eager to have their destiny revealed by the local resident soothsayers. Their horoscopes, as in the West, are based on the date and time of birth, but there all similarity ceases. It is not the movement of the planets which is said to mark our destinies, but their influences, revealed through a series of unceasing cycles. Even at the simplest level, the popular Chinese zodiac of twelve animals is an entirely different concept to the familiar Western one, since it is the year of birth, rather than the birthday, which determines your animal sign.

Chinese astrologers not only reveal a person's prospects for wealth, health, fame and happiness, but also what they can do about it if their future looks none too promising. This part of the book introduces the four factors which rule our destinies according to the traditional Chinese horoscope: the year, month, day and hour of birth. These are analysed in terms of the balance of yin and yang, the twelve animals of the zodiac and the five elements of Chinese philosophy. Once these fundamentals have been set out, the horoscope is ready to reveal the Three Worlds: the past, the present and the future.

THE CHINESE HOROSCOPE

Until a few years ago Chinese astrology was known to the West only through its celebrated zodiac of twelve animals, usually in relation to the year in which a person was born. If this were the case, the flaw in the system would seem to be that everyone born in a particular year would be subject to the same vagaries of fate. There is, of course, more to the Chinese horoscope than the animal signs ruling a person's year of birth (although this does play a central role), as we are about to find out.

In many ways, however, this rough-and-ready interpretation of people's fortunes – putting everyone of a certain age into the same personality group – does have some basis in fact. Any teacher will testify to the fact that each year's intake of students has its own kind of group personality, as distinctly different though each individual might be. There may be universal factors – perhaps the climate, or political circumstances, which might have influenced the childhood of those people and moulded their personality traits. Perhaps, to a certain extent, people are like wines – their vintage depends on the year they were made.

Yet there are three other crucial factors involved in the compilation of a Chinese horoscope. Marco Polo mentioned this in his famous account of his travels through Mongolia and China. Although, as we shall see later, he had a somewhat confused notion of the Chinese zodiac, he must have seen an example of an actual Chinese horoscope since he remarked on one of its chief distinctive characteristics: 'When an astrologer wishes to compile the horoscope of someone, he asks them for the year, the month, the day, and the hour of birth.' That is a puzzling statement. Western astrologers also need to know the date and time of birth to compile a horoscope, as Marco Polo would have known, so why mention it as if it was something curious? But yet he specifies the fact that they ask for these four factors: the year, month, day and hour.

THE FOUR COLUMNS

In the traditional Chinese horoscope, these four divisions of the date would be written at the head of four columns, Chinese (and Mongolian) writing being written vertically, top to bottom. Thus, the Chinese refer to the basic data of the horoscope as the 'Four Columns'. (Most Western writers have adopted the term 'Four Pillars' for these features – the word for 'column' and 'pillar' is the same in the original Chinese.) Also, as each of the four time factors (year, month, day and hour) is expressed in time by two Chinese characters – the *stem* and the *branch* – so the Four Columns are also known as the Eight Characters.

It used to be a traditional Chinese custom that, when a family wished to arrange a marriage, the young man would send a card to his intended inscribed with his Eight Characters. If the family wished to decline the proposal, the card was returned with the sad information that the horoscopes of the couple were not compatible. If, on the other hand, the proposal was accepted, the card would be returned together with the Eight Characters of the bride-to-be added to it.

When Chinese astrology first started to become popular in the West, the few books then available on the subject seemed to be confined almost entirely to descriptions of the twelve personality types of the Chinese zodiac. But now, with a growing interest in this fascinating subject, the time is right for a chance to look into the Chinese horoscope in greater depth.

THE CHINESE CALENDAR

One of the great stumbling blocks in the way of a deeper appreciation of Chinese astrology is its reliance on the very complex Chinese calendar. The Chinese use several calendars simultaneously. One calendar is based on the phases of the Moon, which is why the Chinese celebrate the New Year on a different day each year. Additionally, each day is counted off, not only by the seven days of the week, but also by the ten days of an ancient Chinese week (the stems), another 'week' of twelve days (the branches), and another of a mixture of twelve and thirteen days, and finally by dividing the year itself into twenty-four equal parts of about fifteen days. They also use our own Western calendar.

When it comes to reckoning a person's horoscope, there are as many ways of reckoning the start of the year as there are calendars. Even established astrologers in China find themselves in dispute over the start of the year, often leading to heated debate between the various rival schools of thought.

The reason for all the confusion is that the ancient Chinese calendar, based on the phases of the Moon, was of no use to astronomers, who wanted to take accurate measurements of the sky. They therefore needed to have a calendar that was based on the more predictable movements of the Earth round the Sun, rather than those of the Moon round the Earth. Both calendars, however, were needed for the astronomers to be able to predict eclipses – regarded in those days as an event of dire omen. A failure to predict an eclipse would mean that the necessary rituals could not be performed in sufficient time to avert disaster. The Chinese classics are full of tales of the terrible consequences following eclipses which had not been ceremoniously celebrated.

Those of us who have been brought up on the Western calendar have been sheltered from these academic problems, since our own calendar is, astronomically, about as accurate as it is possible to be. In fact, the only problem is that once every four years an extra day has to be added to keep up with the apparent movements of the Heavens.

Knowing these problems and, more importantly, the fundamental reasons for the controversy, means that the disputes and confusion arising from the multitude of Chinese calendars can be solved very easily by the simple expedient of using the Western calendar as the cornerstone for building the Four Columns of the Chinese horoscope. With the tables given in the chart booklet contained within this pack, the Four Columns – for all but the most hairline cases of birthdate and time – can be calculated correctly and unambiguously. If, however, your own birth data should fall on the knife edge between two possibilities, then you are obviously a very special person who needs to draw up two horoscopes to see which suits you best. You are likely to find a bit of both in you.

THE FORMAT

Before selecting the format for the horoscope chart used in this kit, careful study was made of a wide range of different horoscope charts spanning a period of two thousand years. These charts came from different provinces of China, as well as from other parts of the Eastern world, including Japan, Thailand, Tibet, Mongolia and Siberia. Some of these were thousand-year-old manuscripts compiled by monks laboriously poring over their pages in the monastery caves of central China. Others were rare woodcut illustrations in the priceless collection of books in the British Library. Still others were nothing more than copies of rough sketches made by unlettered mendicants who travelled

Why use cards?

As we saw earlier, each of the Four Columns is made up of a stem and a branch. The stems relate to the five elements of Chinese astrology (Wood, Fire, Earth, Metal, Water) and the branches relate to the twelve animals. The horoscope cards provided allow you simply to piece together the animals and elements relating to each column, using the easy-to-follow instructions, giving you a complete horoscope chart made up of eight cards. This unique system allows for immediate visual analysis of the horoscope, as you can see at a glance the balance of animals, elements and yin and yang within the chart. Using your chart as reference, you can then interpret the personality profile, gaining insight into the person's strengths and weaknesses, their compatibility with others, and the influence of their animals and elements on various life areas, including family, career and wealth. You will be able to forecast that person's future, using the ten-year cycles of fate, and discover lucky and unlucky days for a whole host of everyday activities.

Westerners new to Chinese astrology generally think of their Year Animal as the central feature of their horoscope. Indeed, this is also the case for Chinese parents wanting to find suitable partners for their offspring. This being so, the card for the Year Animal is placed here in its prime position at the centre of the horoscope chart – a visual anchor which relates to the seven other horoscope factors. The choice of the seven-sided chart format has further significance within the realms of Chinese astrology, other than ease of accessibility. The Chinese classics state that our destinies are ruled by the Seven Regulators, these being either the Sun, Moon and five planets of astronomy, or – as in this case – yang, yin and the five elements of astrology.

through Asia with a knapsack of tattered cloth charts and coloured beads for counting.

Nearly all of these charts had one thing in common, however. They were designed for the astrologer's use. To the client, they would be as meaningless – and about as useful – as an alien astronaut's flight plan. However, the aim of this astrology pack is not to mystify, but to make the horoscope communicate as clearly as possible. To this end, a hint was taken from those early Buddhist pioneers who had so carefully devised the wonderful series of animal names to make their horoscopes, and interpretation, more accessible to their clientele.

For our use, then, it was necessary to reshape the format of the horoscope, just as many astrologers in different states and at different times had done before. Some astrologers might prefer a round format; others, a square one. Indeed, at around the same time that Western astrologers dispensed with the old-fashioned square 'Indian' horoscope chart, preferring instead the more practical circular one, Chinese astrologers gave up their circular charts to adopt the square Indian system. Again, the 'Four Column' structure, convenient and practical for Mongolian and Chinese writing – which runs from top to bottom – is an uncomfortable format for those of us who write from side to side. This is where the heptagonal format devised for this pack really comes into its own.

The panel to the left shows an example of how your horoscope chart will look once you've pieced together the cards relating to your birth details. As you will see, the card system is invaluable when it comes to interpreting the meaning of your chart.

THE INTERPRETATIONS

Following the compilation of the horoscope chart, the next stage is its interpretation. The methods of analysing and interpreting the horoscope described in this book are soundly based on classical Chinese examples. In addition, all the explanations of the meanings of signs, elements and correspondences, included in Part Two, have been based on passages in ancient classical Chinese writing.

The historical facts contained in the introduction to the twelve animals and the five elements included on the following pages provides important insight into the interpretation of the horoscopes. While it is interesting to know the personality profiles of the Dragon or the Dog, or the characteristic qualities of someone who has a lot of Fire in their horoscope, for example, it is more important for the serious student to know the reasoning and understanding that gave rise to these observations.

With this solid foundation, and the wisdom of experience, the aspiring reader of Chinese horoscopes needs only one further thing. To quote the opening words from the Confucian Analects:

What can be more rewarding than constant study and practice?
CONFUCIAN ANALECTS

學而是習之
不亦說乎

11

THE TWELVE ANIMALS

The most familiar aspect of Chinese astrology is its zodiac of twelve animals. It is an obvious point of departure between the Western and the Chinese systems of popular astrology since, in the West, when someone asks your zodiac sign, they want to know what month you were born in; in Chinese astrology, it is the year in which you were born that determines your Chinese zodiac sign.

The twelve animal signs, from Rat to Pig, are not Chinese versions of the Western zodiac, and it is a mistake to try to correlate the two. 'I'm a Sagittarius – what's that in the Chinese zodiac?' is a question that can't be answered. Both systems have twelve signs, of which the second – Taurus, or the Ox – is the same. But there the similarity ends.

Because Westerners like to determine character and temperament from their zodiac sign, it has become popular to do the same with Chinese zodiac signs. But the 'animal' characteristics must not be taken too literally. The twelve animal names are actually quite a recent addition to Chinese astrology, and were invented to help astrologers remember the characteristics of each sign. For example, the distinguishing qualities of the Dog type – fidelity and defensiveness – are not derived from the characteristics of a dog. Rather, the name of the Dog was chosen because this was the animal which best summed up those particular features. As we go deeper into the fascinating world of the Chinese horoscope, the animal names will be seen to be a useful tool in helping to remember and understand the potential of the twelve signs. But it is just as important for the astrologer to understand the original meaning of the signs before the happy invention of the twelve animal names.

THE TWELVE BRANCHES

Before we consider the significance of the twelve animals, it is worth taking a look at the astrological system used in China thousands of years before the animal names were introduced. As early as written records began, the Chinese used a system of reckoning time in periods of twelve – like our twelve months – called the 'twelve branches'. Originally, the branches marked the twelve 'watches' or two-hour periods of the day. For the first of these, indicating midnight, there was a sign representing a baby to signify the birth of a new day. Midday was shown by a pair of scales, balancing the first and second halves of the day. Six o'clock in the morning, dawn, was indicated by the rising sun, while six o'clock at night, dusk, was represented by a wine bottle – suggesting a welcome drink at the end of a day's work. But over the course of time these signs became stylized, and their original meanings forgotten.

At a very early period in Chinese history, the twelve branches were also used to number the days. Then, because there were twelve months in the year, the months were also numbered by these twelve branches. Curiously, however, what is now the most common function of the branches – for counting the years – was the last aspect of the date to be reckoned in this way. In former times, this was calculated by the length of time the emperor had been on the throne. But, by reckoning with the twelve branches, one did not need such historical knowledge. Today, as for a thousand or so years, all Chinese calendars and almanacs show the branch for the year, month and day.

ENTER THE TWELVE ANIMALS

After thousands of years, the twelve-branch system gave way to the now familiar zodiac of twelve animals: Rat, Ox, Tiger, Rabbit, Dragon, Snake, Horse, Sheep, Monkey, Rooster, Dog and Pig.

Strangely, the 'Chinese zodiac' may not be Chinese at all. Kurdish shepherds in Iraq and Iran use the names to count the years, and in Turkey there is an ancient ceremonial gate which has the twelve animals carved on it. On the other side of Asia, sculptures of the twelve animals guarded the tombs of the kings of Korea. Perhaps the twelve animals were tribal totems originating among the horse-riding nomads of Central Asia. Marco Polo remarked on them in the journal he compiled on his visit to the Great Khan around 1370. Writing about the local customs, he estimated that there were about five thousand astrologers working in the city, referring, rather inaccurately, to their zodiac: 'The first is the sign of the Lion, the second the Ox, the third the Dragon, the fourth the Dog, and so on, up to twelve.' At least he managed to get one of these statements right.

Two thousand years ago, however, the twelve animals seem to have been unknown to Chinese writers: the great Chinese astronomer, Sima Qian, who lived in the first century BCE, made no mention of them. Then, around the eighth century CE, the animal zodiac began appearing in literature and art throughout the whole of Asia, from east to west. The idea was probably introduced by Buddhist monks from India, who earned their keep by compiling horoscopes. But the old Chinese signs were incomprehensible and featureless. Replacing the Chinese algebraic 'branches' with animal imagery was a masterstroke of invention and spread throughout Asia. Although this didn't completely dispel the need to understand the old system of branches, it certainly helped to make it easier to remember their significance.

RELATIONSHIPS

The people of China often derive amusement by matching potential couples by their zodiac signs. Indeed, young men and women are often warned against furthering their marriage prospects if the signs are not right. Many Chinese proverbs offer advice on this crucial step in life. These include: 'Never bring a Tigress into the house'; 'Ox and Horse never share the same stable'; and, more favourably, 'When the Rabbit meets the Snake, there is true happiness.'

FAVOURABLE TIMES

The pairing of couples in this way is an example of the fact that the Chinese are very down-to-earth in their approach to astrology. The idea that the animal sign determines personality is not as important to them as its practical application. Although the Western world likes to think of the personal characteristics of each animal type, the Chinese would rather know what the useful benefits will be. Because each sign represents a year, rather than a month, it is possible to make a forecast of what the coming year is likely to have in store in matters of health, wealth, career and happiness. When the horoscope is delved into yet further, it is also possible to calculate the prospects of longer or shorter periods of time, and discover whether certain months, days or times are favourable.

THE SIX HOUSES OF THE ANIMALS

The twelve animals form six pairs – yang and yin – and live in six houses which have an important bearing on their interpretation in the horoscope. The Six Houses are Creativity, Development, Spirituality, Sexuality, Career and Home Life. These are shown in the table below, and their significance explained more fully in the introductory paragraphs to each animal sign in Part Two.

THE SIX HOUSES OF THE TWELVE ANIMALS

Animal	Yang/Yin	House	Significance
Rat	Yang	Creativity	The Rat is the starter
Ox	Yin		The Ox is the finisher
Tiger	Yang	Development	The Tiger conquers by force
Rabbit	Yin		The Rabbit conquers by diplomacy
Dragon	Yang	Spirituality	The Dragon is the magician
Snake	Yin		The Snake is the mystic
Horse	Yang	Sexuality	The Horse represents masculine
Sheep	Yin		The Sheep represents feminine
Monkey	Yang	Career	The Monkey has dexterity
Rooster	Yin		The Rooster has flair
Dog	Yang	Home Life	The Dog builds
Pig	Yin		The Pig furnishes

How to Interpret the Twelve Animals

The twelve animals are described in Part Two, along with their effect in the horoscope. Each animal description is divided into five sections for ease of interpretation.

1 Meaning of the sign An introduction to the original meaning of the sign, before the twelve animal names were invented. This explains the basic symbolism and influence of that sign, as a guide to personality traits, and to allow interpretation of the horoscope in greater detail.

2 Personality The animal for the year of birth is the first factor in determining personality traits and character. In popular Chinese astrology, this is the equivalent of Western zodiac sign astrology.

3 Compatibility The compatibility of two people can be assessed by comparing their Year Animal signs. Done for marriage or for business partners.

4 Favourable periods Comparing the Year Animal with that of any given year (or day, month or longer period) gives a rough appraisal of whether the year (or equivalent) is going to be favourable or not.

5 Influences of other animals Once the animal signs for month, day and hour have been calculated, a deeper assessment of potential can be made by comparing the four animals in the horoscope chart. There are also specific combinations of signs that have a bearing on the horoscope (*see right*).

SPECIAL ANIMAL COMBINATIONS

Certain combinations – in pairs, threes and fours – are particularly favourable or unfavourable. For example, the combination of Ox, Snake and Rooster indicates a strong business sense, whereas a pairing of Rat and Horse could suggest inner conflict. These groupings are known as the Four Triangles and the Three Crosses, (see below), and

quick-reference diagrams are included on pages 2–3 of the chart booklet. There are also two signs to look out for: the Post Horse, which shows the person is likely to travel far and move abroad, and the Flower of Love, which may lead to happiness or self-destruction (these two signs are indicated in section 5 of each animal description). But the signs only indicate what roads lay open ahead; the route we take is of our own doing.

| *The Four Triangles* These groups of three signs form a close affinity, and this is regarded as extremely favourable in a horoscope chart. | *Triangle of Creativity* NORTH / *Water* RAT • DRAGON • MONKEY When these three are present, it reveals inventive genius and inspired people who are able to make their ideas work. | *Triangle of Trade and Commerce* WEST / *Metal* OX • SNAKE • ROOSTER This reveals good business sense, and the ability to make and promote manufactured products. There is potential to become wealthy. | *Triangle of Ambition* SOUTH / *Fire* TIGER • HORSE • DOG The three hunters indicate a strongly motivated person, who is determined to succeed at all costs. | *Triangle of Home and Family* EAST / *Wood* RABBIT • SHEEP • PIG These three signs show a rich and fruitful career, and satisfaction at having lived a happy and contented life. |

| *The Three Crosses* When two signs form opposite pairs, such as the Rat and Horse, they are considered unfavourable and antagonistic to each other. Other unfavourable combinations occur when there are two intervening signs between them, such | as Rat and Rabbit. To have two or three such signs in a chart would signify a problem to be resolved. But when all four unfavourable signs are together, this not only eliminates the problem, but introduces a new, highly positive feature. | *The Four Flowers of Love* THE FOUR DIRECTIONS RAT • RABBIT • HORSE • ROOSTER Power and fame. This group signifies balance through tension. The horoscope of the great Qian Long Emperor had these four signs. | *The Literary Cross* THE FOUR EARTH SIGNS OX • DRAGON • SHEEP • DOG Literary and artistic merit. This group reveals artistic potential. J. S. Bach had these four signs in his horoscope. | *The Four Coaching Posts* THE FOUR ELEMENTS TIGER • SNAKE • MONKEY • PIG Travel and emigration. This group signifies continuous travel – a nomadic life, or emigration (either voluntary or obligatory). |

Missing Signs

If three animal signs from one cross are present, and one missing, one aspect of life may be adversely affected (see chart booklet, page 3, for specific areas affected). This problem

can be resolved during a time period governed by the missing animal sign. Another solution would be a partnership with someone who has the missing sign as their Year Animal, though normally considered unfavourable.

THE FIVE ELEMENTS

The five elements of Chinese philosophy – Wood, Fire, Earth, Metal and Water – lie at the core of Chinese science and aesthetics. These elements are familiar to followers of feng shui, where they are revealed by shapes, colours and other aspects of the environment. In Chinese astrology, they are revealed by time factors – the hour, day, month and year.

Just as each year has its own zodiac animal sign, so each year also belongs to one of the elements. For example, the years 1989 and 2001 are Snake years; but 1989 is an Earth Snake year and 2001 a Metal Snake year. The personality type of a particular zodiac sign is made more specific by using both the animal sign and element. For example, Fire Horse types are more reactionary than their creative Wood Horse colleagues. And, just as every year can be described by an animal and an element, so too can the months, days and hours. These are the essential fundamentals for compiling and interpreting the Chinese horoscope.

THE ORIGIN OF THE FIVE ELEMENTS

According to legend, knowledge of the five elements was brought to the people by the spirits of the planets Jupiter, Mars, Saturn, Venus and Mercury, riding on five rams. Each ram was a different colour – green, red, yellow, white and black – signifying the five elements, and held in its mouth a grain: these became the first crops of the Chinese people. On touching the ground, the rams were turned to stone.

The legend has an unexpected significance. The first listing of the five elements occurs in the Chinese classic, the *Shu Jing* (Book II, ch. 1, v. 7) where they are described as the five essentials for growing crops – water, sunlight and earth, and wood and metal for tools.

CHINESE AND WESTERN ASTROLOGY

The connection between the five elements and the five inner planets underlines the essential difference between the Chinese concept of five elements and the Western concept of four. Although three of the names are the same, there are no other similarities.

The Wood element is associated with Jupiter and, as the element of spring, rebirth and creativity, is considered to be the most feminine of the elements. Venus, the 'female' planet in the West, is known to the Chinese as the Metal planet, because it glitters and shines like polished steel. Because it is associated with autumn, ploughing, sharp instruments and swords, it is regarded as the masculine planet. The other three planetary elements are: the Earth planet, Saturn; the Fire planet, Mars; and the Water planet, Mercury.

The colours of the elements are taken from the actual hues of their respective planets. We have already noted that Mars, the Fire planet, is red, and that Venus (Metal) is a steely white. Of the other planets, Jupiter (Wood) has a bluish-green tinge, and Saturn (Earth) has a yellow appearance. Mercury (another white planet) seems to be allocated the colour black by default. However, the observation is that water, when not reflecting the sky, appears black. (*See chart booklet, page 4, for a summary of element attributes.*)

SEQUENCES OF THE ELEMENTS

Far more important, however, is the function of two specific sequences, since this has been their determinative role in feng shui, astrology, Chinese medicine and virtually every aspect of social and court life throughout Chinese history.

The Productive Cycle

The five elements are normally written in their 'productive' sequence: Wood–Fire–Earth–Metal–Water, and back to Wood to begin the cycle again. Wood burns, producing fire; Fire leaves ash (the earth) behind; From the earth we extract metal; metal can be melted and made to flow like water; and water is needed to make plants (wood) grow.

Each element in the sequence is said to be the 'mother' of the next. Thus, Metal is the mother of Water, while Wood is the child of Water. Two elements that are in a mother-and-child relationship are in harmony. Therefore, Fire and Wood are in harmony, even though it may seem that Fire burns Wood. A mother looks after her child, and gives it love, without asking anything in return. But children need their mothers, and will run to them when they are afraid. When an element is weak or missing, it needs its 'mother' to support it.

Since particular elements represent a person's health, wealth, success, career or happiness, it is important to ensure that the elements are balanced – not just with respect to the horoscope, but also to the events and people in that person's life. For example, if someone's horoscope showed that the 'wealth' was in Earth, we could expect wealth to grow during a Fire year, since Fire is the mother of Earth, then remain steady during an Earth year, but be distributed (although beneficially) during a Metal year, Earth being the mother of Metal.

The Destructive Cycle

This is formed by taking every alternate element in the productive sequence: Wood–Earth–Water–Fire–Metal, and back to Wood to continue the cycle. Wood destroys earth by taking all the goodness out; earth pollutes water, making it unfit for drinking or washing; water puts out fire; fire melts metal; and metal chops down wood.

The destructive elements produce their effects in different ways. Although growing plants (Wood) exhausts the earth, it can be fertilized and made fruitful again. Earth might pollute water, but it will settle, and in time the water will be fresh again. And, although fire might melt metal, when the fire ceases, the metal regains it strength. Metal is used to chop down wood, but for a purpose, as the wood is made into useful things. But when water puts out fire, the fire is out. However, when two elements are in a destructive position there are ways to rectify the situation. The problem is reduced if there is a 'buffer' element in between. For example, in the case of the Wood element threatening Earth, the situation will be remedied if the intervening element – Fire – is present, as the 'mother' of Earth, the element under threat. A Chinese astrologer will take these effects into account when examining a horoscope.

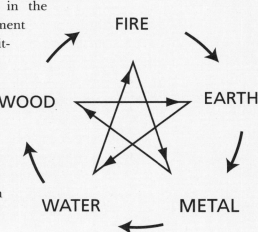

The productive cycle of elements is shown in the outer circle, and the destructive cycle in the inner pentagram.

YANG AND YIN ELEMENTS

When the elements, in their productive sequence, are used to designate the years, months, days and hours, they proceed in pairs; for example, the years 2000 and 2001 are both Metal years, 2002 and 2003 Water years, and so on. The first element of each pair is *yang*, and the second *yin*. To distinguish between the two types of elements, some people identify the yang and yin qualities with distinguishing names – Yang Wood being hard and firm like pine trees, for instance, and Yin Wood like grass or herbs. These names (see separate sections on each element in Part Two) are helpful for remembering the qualities of the elements.

The expression 'yin and yang' refers to two forces that are inseparable, like the negative and positive poles of a battery. Unfortunately, in everyday language the words positive and negative suggest good and bad, which is misleading. Yin is what yang is not. There can be no yang without yin.

The words 'yin' and 'yang' were first recorded in a poem describing the sunny and shaded sides of a hill. The men worked outside in the sun, while the women remained in the shaded house; thus 'yang' came to mean not only sunny, but male, and yin female. In Chinese literature, the Sun is known as the Great Yang, and the Moon the Great Yin.

In Chinese philosophy, yang signifies activity and forward movement, while yin represents the receiver or stillness. Yang starts, yin finishes. The five elements have both yang and yin qualities, while six of the zodiac animals are yang and the other six yin. When the horoscope is examined in finer detail, the matching of yang and yin signs is often a significant factor in its interpretation.

YANG	YIN
Sun	*Moon*
Male	*Female*
Heaven	*Earth*
Rising	*Falling*
Outside	*Inside*
Odd	*Even*
Sending	*Receiving*
Moving	*Remaining*

THE SEASONS

The five elements are associated with the cardinal points – north, east, south and west – and the centre. These are associated with the four seasons, the exception being Earth, which rules the last eighteen days of each season. Thus Wood rules the spring, when life is beginning; Fire the summer, when the sun is at its height; Metal the autumn, when harvesting is carried out; and Water the cold Winter.

If a person's year element matches that of the season in which they are born, or is supported by it, it is considered very favourable. Thus, it is a favourable sign if someone is born in a Metal year in the autumn, but less favourable for someone born in the summer of the same year, since the element for summer is Fire, which melts Metal. However, it is more important to be aware of the 'inner' element present in every animal sign.

BRANCH ELEMENTS OF THE ANIMALS

Each animal has its own element, or *branch element*, which never changes – no matter what the day, month, year or season. For example, the fixed element for the Horse is Fire. So, people born in those years already have Fire in their horoscopes, while those born in a Fire Horse year have a double helping (the branch element for the Horse *and* the element relating to a particular year) – even before the month, day and hour are considered. As a second example, the branch element for Dragon is Earth, but the year 2000 was a Metal year. Metal is the 'external' (changing) element, and Earth the fixed element. The branch elements for the animal signs are listed in the animal section in Part Two.

How to Interpret the Five Elements

The five elements are described in Part Two, along with their effect in the horoscope. As with the animals, each element description is divided into sections, for ease of interpretation.

1 General qualities Firstly there is an introduction to the meaning of the element – its general qualities and associations, and what it represents.

2 Personality In popular astrology, the elemental personality type is based on the year of birth, just as for the animal sign, which it supplements. These two opening sections together provide a brief character sketch, and can be referred to as soon as the element for the year of birth is known.

3 Element weighting Having laid out all the cards and completed the horoscope chart, the 'weighting' for each element can be seen. This gives an indication of the element qualities of the person, but its main function is to evaluate the strengths of the 'happinesses' (*see also section 5, below*). You will also be able to gauge the balance of elements in the chart, and whether there are any unfavourable or discordant element combinations.

4 How to revitalize an element The element weighting reveals whether there is a balance of elements in the horoscope chart. If you find that certain elements need supporting or strengthening (perhaps they may be overpowered by other elements in the chart), or that missing elements need to be introduced to achieve a balance, this section shows you how.

5 Meaning of other elements The Five Happinesses – health, wealth, career, recognition and family satisfaction – are related to the 'personal', or day, element. The element weighting reveals their strengths, and can also reveal whether a particular aspect of happiness is in a strong position or a weakened state. This section highlights important factors to look for in the horoscope, and what they mean. By comparing the associated element with elements of particular dates, it is possible to see when that aspect of life may be improved, or when it may be likely to be in a difficult situation.

SPECIFIC QUESTIONS

You can also use the elements to help solve specific problems. To seek the answer to a problem, decide which element is suited to the type of question. For example, the Wood element refers to family matters (*see 'Activity' entry in chart on page 4 of chart booklet*). Then, from the tables, find the element for the period under consideration. Compare the two elements to see whether they are harmonious, favourable or unsympathetic. This process is used by Chinese astrologers to calculate favourable days.

For particular problems, it is possible to see if one's Day Element favours oneself or a particular subject. Perhaps the *time factor* element favours the theme of enquiry, but not the person asking. For instance, suppose someone whose Day Element was Fire wished to ask about family matters (belonging to Wood) and the day in question was Water. This would mean that in any dispute about family matters the outcome would be favourable for the family, but not for the enquirer personally, since Water (the *time*) feeds Wood (the *question*), but quenches Fire (the *enquirer*).

CYCLES OF FATE

*The*he earliest known examples of Chinese writing are found on 'oracle bones'. These are relics of the ancient astrologer's art, for they are the remains of observations made by the astronomer-astrologer, together with the questions asked, the astrologer's answers and, often, an added remark to say whether the prediction had happened as foretold. Yet what makes these 'oracle bones' so historically important is that they often had the date inscribed on them as well. The date was recorded by a calendar system still in use today in China and many other countries of the Far East – the curiously named 'stems and branches'.

THE STEMS AND BRANCHES

We have already met the branches, although by a different name: the twelve animal signs of the now familiar Chinese zodiac. The stems are even older. They were the first time-markers ever used by the Chinese, and were originally the names of the days of a ten-day week. Just as our own days of the week are named after pagan gods, it is likely that the ten stems were the names of ancient gods who have now been virtually forgotten.

The sequences of stems and branches repeat continuously to produce the Cycle of Sixty.

THE CYCLE OF SIXTY

At an early date in Chinese history, the system of counting the days by the ten stems was refined by counting the days in twelves as well as tens, thus using the twelve branches as well. This produced a cycle of sixty possible combinations: the ten stems and twelve branches repeat in a continuous cycle, producing sixty different pairings (the stems repeat five times and the branches six times, before the cycle begins again with the first pairing). This sounds more complex than it is – the table below should help to make it clear. NOTE: The stems are usually written as Arabic numbers, and the branches as Roman numerals.

Yin and Yang Elements
The stems and branches are still used by the Chinese in their own calendars and diaries, but about a thousand years ago, astrologers coming to China from the West found this system too difficult for people who could not read and write to understand. The twelve animal names having been a happy invention, the next step was to find an easier alternative for the ten stems. The solution was simply to give them the names of their associated elements, with the appropriate yang or yin label to identify whether they were odd- or even-numbered stems (*see table right*). For example, what

POSITION IN SERIES	1	2	3	4	5	6	7	8	9	10	11	12	13	14	15	16	17	18	19	20	21	22	23	24	25	26	27...
STEM	1	2	3	4	5	6	7	8	9	10	1	2	3	4	5	6	7	8	9	10	1	2	3	4	5	6	7...
BRANCH	I	II	III	IV	V	VI	VII	VIII	IX	X	XI	XII	I	II	III	IV	V	VI	VII	VIII	IX	X	XI	XII	I	II	III...

used to be called 'Stem 1' in the Chinese calendar could now be referred to as 'Yang Wood', 'Stem 4' as 'Yin Fire', and so on. The branches and corresponding animals are also shown below. (The complete Cycle of Sixty is shown in the chart booklet, page 5.)

The Hours, Months and Years
About two thousand years ago, the double numbering of the days by the stems and branches was adopted for the years. Much later, the new system of element and animal names was introduced for counting years and this became the official way of recording the date in the outposts of China, particularly in Mongolia and Tibet. Ordinary folk used the animal names for the hours, too, although the element label was not in general use. Similarly, even in official documents, the months of the year did not need to have an extra stem-and-branch tag, since they were clearly related to the natural seasonal terms of the year.

But, for the astrologer, the stem and branch of the hour, day, month and year were important, as the traveller Marco Polo had observed. The horoscopes that he saw in China and Mongolia were probably drawn up according to the 'new' system, using the element for the stem and the animal sign for the branch, since he mentioned animals by name. Now that you are familiar with the stems and branches, you are ready to compile – and interpret – your horoscope chart, using the cards in this pack. The following pages will show you how. Below is a quick reminder of the components of the Four Columns – the basis of your horoscope.

THE FOUR COLUMNS OF FATE

As we have already discovered, these form the foundations of the Chinese horoscope. To sum up:

- The columns consist of the year, month, day and hour of birth.
- Each column is represented by two factors: a stem and a branch.
- A stem can be expressed by an element with its polarity – yang or yin.
- A branch can be expressed by an animal zodiac sign.
- Additionally, each animal zodiac sign has its own branch element, which never changes.

MODERN CHINESE	甲	乙	丙	丁	戊	己	庚	辛	壬	癸
STEM	1	2	3	4	5	6	7	8	9	10
ELEMENT	WOOD		FIRE		EARTH		METAL		WATER	
YANG OR YIN	Yang	Yin	Yang	Yin	Yang	Yin	Yang	Yin	Yang	Yin

MODERN CHINESE	子	丑	寅	卯	辰	巳	午	未	申	酉	戌	亥
BRANCH	I	II	III	IV	V	VI	VII	VIII	IX	X	XI	XII
ANIMAL	RAT	OX	TIGER	RABBIT	DRAGON	SNAKE	HORSE	SHEEP	MONKEY	ROOSTER	DOG	PIG
YANG OR YIN	Yang	Yin	Yang	Yin	Yang	Yin	Yang	Yin	Yang	Yin	Yang	Yin

The stems and branches translate into the elements and animals for modern-day use.

Part Two

COMPILING AND INTERPRETING A HOROSCOPE

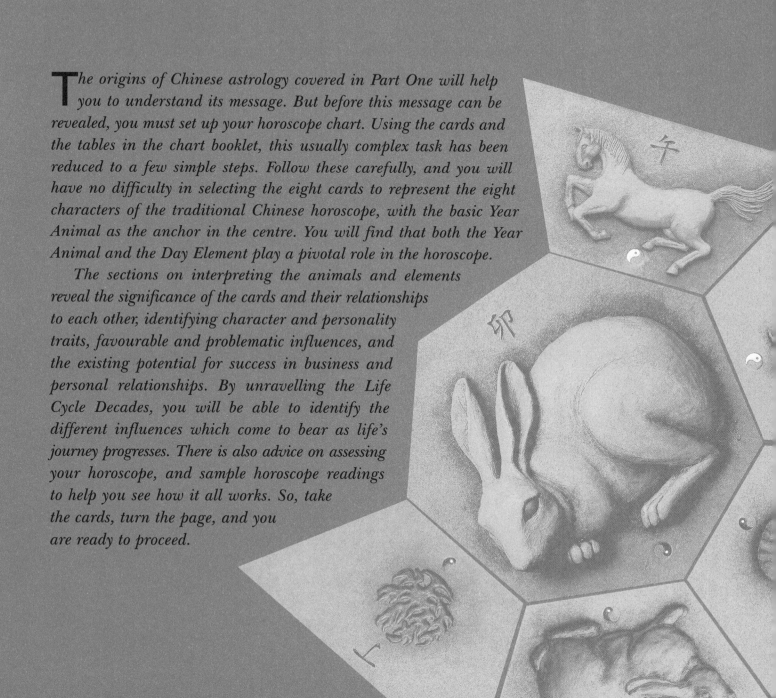

The origins of Chinese astrology covered in *Part One* will help you to understand its message. But before this message can be revealed, you must set up your horoscope chart. Using the cards and the tables in the chart booklet, this usually complex task has been reduced to a few simple steps. Follow these carefully, and you will have no difficulty in selecting the eight cards to represent the eight characters of the traditional Chinese horoscope, with the basic Year Animal as the anchor in the centre. You will find that both the Year Animal and the Day Element play a pivotal role in the horoscope.

The sections on interpreting the animals and elements reveal the significance of the cards and their relationships to each other, identifying character and personality traits, favourable and problematic influences, and the existing potential for success in business and personal relationships. By unravelling the Life Cycle Decades, you will be able to identify the different influences which come to bear as life's journey progresses. There is also advice on assessing your horoscope, and sample horoscope readings to help you see how it all works. So, take the cards, turn the page, and you are ready to proceed.

HOW TO SET UP YOUR HOROSCOPE CHART

A Chinese horoscope is said to be supported on Four Columns – the four divisions of the birthdate: year, month, day and hour. In the horoscope chart you are about to compile, each column is represented by two cards: an animal sign and a stem element. The animal sign for the year of birth is placed in the centre of the chart – the anchor – and the remaining seven cards are built up around it. Follow the simple step-by-step instructions below and piece the cards together as shown to complete your chart. (NOTE: The cards are double-sided and cater for all horoscope permutations. If you can't find the card you need, you may need to swap one of the ones you have already used.)

The birth details for Diana, Princess of Wales, are used here as an example.
Date of birth: 1 July 1961   Time: 07:45 local time (England)

1 THE FIRST COLUMN

This refers to the animal and element for the **year** of birth. To find out your details, turn to Chart 1 on page 6 in the chart booklet (make sure you read the note accompanying the chart, as this has a bearing on which year – according to the Chinese calendar – applies to your birthdate). Then, find the corresponding horoscope cards and position them as shown (you need to use one of the seven-sided cards for the Year Animal, as this forms the central 'anchor' in your chart).

EXAMPLE: *The year of birth was 1961. From Chart 1 we see that the Year Animal is Ox and the Year Stem Element is Yin Metal.*

2 THE SECOND COLUMN

This refers to the animal and element for the **month** of birth. This is found very simply from Chart 2 on page 8 of the chart booklet (again, read the note accompanying the chart). Once you have looked up the information, find the corresponding horoscope cards and add them to your chart.

EXAMPLE: *The date of birth was 1 July. From Chart 2 we see that the Month Animal is Horse and the Month Stem Element is Yang Wood.*

Your Complete Chart

Your horoscope chart is now ready for you to interpret (*see right*). Blank grids are included on page 16 in the chart booklet for you to photocopy, so that you can record the horoscope information each time you do a chart, for future reference. For the animal cards, be sure to note down the element too, since the balance of elements is a vital aspect of interpreting a horoscope. Similarly, also note whether each card is yin or yang, and indicate which element is your personal Fate Element, too.

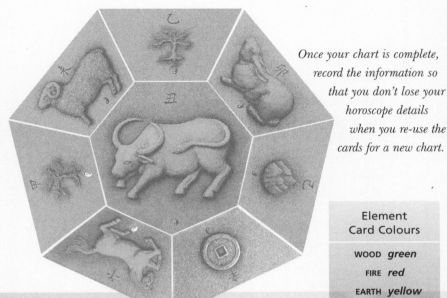

Once your chart is complete, record the information so that you don't lose your horoscope details when you re-use the cards for a new chart.

Element Card Colours	
WOOD	*green*
FIRE	*red*
EARTH	*yellow*
METAL	*silver*
WATER	*blue*

3 THE THIRD COLUMN

This refers to the animal and element for the **day** of birth. The element for this column is particularly important, as it reveals your personal Fate Element, which plays a key role in interpreting the horoscope. To find the animal sign, turn to Chart 3 or 4 on pages 9 or 11 in the booklet (depending on whether or not you were born in a leap year), and to find the element, turn to Chart 5 or 6 on pages 12 or 13. Now add the corresponding cards to your horoscope chart.

4 THE FOURTH COLUMN

This refers to the animal and element for the **hour** of birth. (If you don't know your time of birth, assume that it is midday.) Turn to Chart 7 on page 14 of the booklet for the details, reading the note regarding daylight-saving time adjustments. Then, find the final two corresponding cards and add them to your chart to complete the horoscope. The chart is now ready to be interpreted (the meanings of the animals and elements are included on the following pages). For the interpretation of Diana's chart, see page 90.

EXAMPLE: *The full date of birth is 1 July 1961. Thus from Chart 3 we see that the Day Animal is Sheep, and from Chart 5 that the Day Stem Element is Yin Wood.*

EXAMPLE: *The time of birth was 07:45 local time, with daylight saving in operation – thus 06:45. Chart 7 shows the Hour Animal is Rabbit and the Hour Stem Element is Yin Earth.*

THE RAT

HOUSE: *Creativity*

BRANCH: I / *Yang*

ELEMENT: *Water*

The choice of the Rat to represent the first sign of the Chinese zodiac had nothing to do with any aspect of personality or character. It was because the first sign was believed to indicate the midnight hour, this being the time when these nocturnal creatures are most active. Indeed, the old Chinese sign for the first of the twelve divisions of the day represented a baby, indicating the birth of a new day, or even the start of a new year. Thus, in the Chinese horoscope a Rat sign often means new opportunities.

PERSONALITY

People born in the year of the Rat tend to be thinkers – creative, and enthusiastic about anything new. They are great starters, but less able finishers. They succeed best when they have assistance from someone at their side to encourage them when plans don't seem to work out as well as expected. They tend to be more alert in the late evening rather than earlier in the day, and prefer occupations which can accommodate their preference for unsociable hours. Their personal relationships are complex: friends and acquaintances may find the Rat personality a little mysterious and dark, for they always have 'something of the night' about them. They are good at handling other people's money, but not, alas, their own. For the Rat can be both spendthrift and miserly, alternately hoarding and splashing out, ignoring the option to keep a steady balance in their accounts.

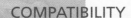

COMPATIBILITY

How people born in the year of the Rat relate to people born in the different animal years

Rat Rat personalities are happy together; they both share each other's needs and foibles. Of course, the relationship may be an open one, but there is considerable mutual support. Faults are understood and excused rather than forgiven. A strong sense of loyalty steers them through the most turbulent troubles.

Ox Every Rat needs an Ox, for the Ox is the true counterpart of the Rat personality. Despite the fact that the Rat may often seem to be the dominant partner, there are many ways – emotionally, physically, and even materially – in which the Ox gains from the fundamental link bonding these two together.

Tiger This combination makes a better commercial partnership than an emotional one. Both have entirely different skills, which can be combined to their mutual advantage. Marriages and other close relationships have greater chance of success when the male is the younger partner; otherwise, there is often a tension below the surface which can erupt into heated dispute.

Rabbit The Rat–Rabbit partnership may be strong on love, but short on passion. Although there may be an outer veneer of understanding between them, there are likely be undercurrents of disquiet. There are unspoken secrets which no one wants to share. It is important to bring problems into the open.

Dragon This relationship brings excitement into romance. There is always a mysterious and unexpected surprise waiting to be sprung. The problem is that with too many surprises such a passionate affair may burn itself out. A steadying influence, or important shared commitment, is needed to seal the bond.

Snake There are aspects of this relationship which are not too comfortable – perhaps there is something unconventional about it which does not meet with general approval. The peak-times of their biological clocks do not agree, so that party-time for one is sleep-time for the other. The danger signs may be seen if the Rat partner looks exhausted and weakened most of the time.

Horse The attraction between these two is more physical than emotional. If they are living together they each need to respect the other partner's need for individuality.

Sheep Quietly going their separate ways, these two could live in the same house for forty years without getting to know each other deeply. They are mutually supportive, nodding encouragement occasionally, saying and doing all the right things, and even remembering anniversaries. And with that they are both perfectly happy.

Monkey This is a lively partner for the fast-thinking Rat. A whirlwind romance, full of sparkle and zest, will lead to a zany and enviable partnership.

The bonds between them are blissfully and firmly cemented.

Rooster Both these individuals are just that – individuals. They need to have their own space, their own ambitions and their own careers. Then, when fully established and confident in their own private world, they can appreciate and respect their partners all the more.

Dog They may not perceive themselves to be the ideal couple, but, when they look round at the problems faced by friends in their relationships, the Rat and Dog realize that they have a lot to be thankful for. Family commitments and other shared interests ensure that this relationship is a steady one.

Pig The Rat being the first sign of the Chinese zodiac, and the Pig the last, shows that this is a relationship that is going to undergo several changes, leading to stress when these changes are unwelcome. The secret of success is being able to combine flexibility with stability.

FAVOURABLE AND UNFAVOURABLE PERIODS

How the Rat fares in periods ruled by the different animal signs

Rat The Rat's own year is an ideal period for innovation and starting afresh, whether this involves moving house, embarking on a new career, or even a new romantic partnership. For shorter-term prospects, the Rat month of December offers fresh opportunities, too.

Ox Ox years are particularly rewarding for Rat personalities, for it is in these years that the Rat begins to reap the benefits of previous achievements. It is a period when help comes from unexpected sources. Commercial activities fare much better.

Tiger Official recognition and help from above are due to the authority of the Tiger. People in high places can be relied upon at last. Projects which have been slow to come to fruition will now be resolved. Spring brings fresh hope.

Rabbit Do not put too much reliance on expecting help from loved ones. They will be looking to you for support, rather than the other way round. There could be a further strain on your financial reserves, though the reasons are worthy and bring you credit.

Dragon A generally perplexing time. There will be unexpected changes, but carefully laid plans may be thwarted. The financial situation fluctuates alarmingly; a windfall will be welcome, but must be offset against sudden demands on resources. Progress will be made, but only after many anxious moments.

Snake A year when it is wise to avoid taking risks and to steer clear of ventures which are not absolutely legitimate. Be prepared for unexpected hazards, and delay caused by ill-health.

Horse The Horse sign is in direct opposition to the Rat. There can be protracted conflicts, especially with regard to personal relationships. In business, disputes and personality clashes make life difficult. Do not be discouraged, as the situation will improve later.

Sheep Although this is an uneventful period, it is one where quiet progress is both productive and psychologically rewarding. Family ties are strengthened, and there will be many opportunities for relaxing and enjoying the finer things in life.

Monkey Renewed vigour gives a feeling of inner strength and confidence. It is a period when you should exert yourself to the full, since you will be rewarded with success in proportion to your efforts, whether your main objectives are career successes or matters of the heart.

Rooster Your self-esteem may suffer a knock-back as a rival comes to the fore. A friend or colleague is likely to take the limelight away from you, which could lead to resentment. But if you stand your ground, patience will be rewarded eventually.

Dog This is a useful period for considering changes to your home. If you decide to move, aim for the south-east – this will bring the greatest benefits.

Pig It is time to consolidate your position. If you are unhappy with your present circumstances, by all means plan for future change, but don't make the move yet. Be happy during this period by making the best of your present circumstances, and improving your environment for the time being.

OTHER ANIMAL INFLUENCES

How the other animal signs in the horoscope chart influence the Rat

Rat A second Rat shows self-confidence and ambition; favourable for money matters and travel. Three or four reveal an inability to communicate with others or see their point of view.

Ox Very favourable: brings self-confidence and reliability, showing inventiveness and the stamina to see things through.

Tiger (Post Horse) Adds determination and authority to the Rat's prospects. Indicates energy, movement and travel.

Rabbit Provides a caring touch, and sympathy for the disadvantaged. Reduces the Rat's usual preference for isolation.

Dragon Draws the Rat to the performing arts and increases the Rat's manipulative skills.

Snake Despite the two signs being unfavourably placed, the Snake shows the greater skill in handling finances. There is a tendency to become withdrawn later in life.

Horse This produces a two-sided personality, torn between entirely different objectives. This individual doesn't want to be thought different. Allergies may be troublesome in middle years.

Sheep This sign neither hinders nor helps the Rat, but it does signify a lack of resources. Such people have to rely on their own efforts. Dreams and ambitions have to be practical.

Monkey This is a very good sign, adding practical skills to intellectual prowess. Witty, and with unusual talents.

Rooster (Flower of Love) This indicates torrid love affairs. Whether male or female, the Rat with the Rooster sign in the horoscope will succeed by developing those skills – practical or converstional – which appeal to women. Marketing, fashion or fiction can be successful career possibilities.

Dog Adds many positive qualities to the Rat's character, indicating an active, popular social life. Such people are likely to be keen on home improvement.

Pig Reduces, to some extent, the Rat's ability to relate to others. A quiet village is preferred to a busy city; and relaxing at home is more enjoyed than hectic socializing.

THE OX

HOUSE: *Creativity*

BRANCH: II / *Yin*

ELEMENT: *Earth*

It may only be a coincidence, but the Ox is the only member of the Chinese zodiac which has the same name, and the same position, as its counterpart in the Western zodiac. But, whereas the sign of Taurus runs from the end of April to the beginning of May, the Chinese Ox month coincides, very nearly, with the month of January.

The Ox is associated with spring, and a picture of the spring Ox appears on the first page of Chinese calendars. Subtle differences in the drawing of the Ox and its bearer tell the readers what the weather is going to be like, whether the year is going to have a good harvest or not, and which grains are likely to fetch the highest prices.

PERSONALITY

People born in the year of the Ox are sturdy and practical types, preferring methods which are known to be serviceable, rather than latching on to the latest fads. The Ox is the yin half of the House of Creativity, and shows a flair for adapting and reshaping what is already well established. The great composer Bach, born in the year of the Ox, revealed his creativity not by novelty but by perfecting the styles which had gone before.

Ox types are not afraid of hard work, and through persistence and determination can overcome the most awesome tasks. Walls built by the Ox will stand for many years.

COMPATIBILITY

How people born in the year of the Ox relate to people born in the different animal years

Rat Being the opposite sides of the same coin, the Ox and Rat form a close bond. Although the Ox may seem to be too deferential to the Rat, the Ox derives stimulus and support from the Rat's innovative input. In romance or business, Rat and Ox can make a successful partnership.

Ox These two are content to stay together with their own family or social group, keeping very much to themselves. Personal relationships are likely to spring from bursts of passion rather than long romances. They make a formidable couple who are unlikely to let obstacles stand in their way.

Tiger The Ox is the one sign that the Tiger tries to avoid. Outside the home, the charismatic Tiger might shine in the adulation of admirers, but the Ox has no such illusions. Behind the drawn curtains of the Ox and Tiger's fashionable home, the Ox is very much in charge.

Rabbit Though the Ox and Rabbit may appear to have entirely different personalities, there is a magnetic attraction which holds these two together. Despite their differences, which may lead to occasional separations, these two are unlikely to remain apart for long. Such a partnership is likely to be blessed with many children.

Dragon The traditionalist Ox and the eccentric Dragon? An unlikely combination. Perhaps both partners are looking for something that is missing in themselves. It is important to keep the purse strings tight.

Snake This could be the ideal partner for the Ox. The magic and mystery of the Dragon that the Ox might find so intriguing is again here in the elegant Snake – but this time it is restrained by the conventional attitudes that the Ox respects. It is also a favourable partnership for a successful business.

Horse The Ox and Horse may share the same field, but they have different stables. The factor missing from this partnership is surprise – an essential ingredient in any romance. But the stability and companionship is very important to them both.

Sheep The Ox must never underestimate the Sheep. It is the one animal of the Chinese zodiac which is able to overcome the seemingly unassailable strength of the Ox. Familiarity must not give way to complacency. The relationship seems to be ever on a knife edge and more understanding is needed.

Monkey Despite the Monkey's manipulative skills, this character is unlikely to impress the cynical Ox. They may not be the ideal couple, but both have ingredients in their psychological make-up which compensate for the shortcomings of the other. With humour on one side, and common sense on the other, this partnership can work.

Rooster Like the Snake, this is another astrologically ideal relationship for the Ox. There is excitement on the one hand, and sound practicality on the other. Mutual support and dependency keep these two in harmony. Whether in a business partnership or a romantic liaison, there is a rich vein of understanding which continually revitalizes this relationship.

Dog For this relationship to succeed, there must be more give and take from both sides. They should occasionally stop to consider what they are doing to make the other person happy, rather than wondering why the other person seems so selfish. It is important for both to understand each other's needs.

Pig This partnership suggests both a happy home life, and an orderly business partnership. There is a keenness for life to be more comfortable, coupled with the determination to make it so. The joys and setbacks of life are shared and, when one has problems, the other listens sympathetically – not just with understanding, but with practical support.

FAVOURABLE AND UNFAVOURABLE PERIODS

How the Ox fares in periods ruled by the different animal signs

Rat Rat years are constructive for Oxen. They may be periods of upheaval and hard work, but the results are beneficial. In Rat months, look for positive signs and clues as to your next move.

Ox Matters may come to a halt during the years of the Ox itself; but the benefits of earlier activity should now start to become evident. Do not use force to try to unblock matters which have become stuck: they will become loose of their own accord.

Tiger There are likely to be problems with people in authority, or government departments. However, despite the odds being stacked against you, you have right on your side and will succeed in the end. Persevere.

Rabbit This is a year for family celebration. Good news will dispel the clouds of gloom that seem to have been hovering over you recently. For the Ox, the Rabbit month (March, but before Easter) is a favourable time either for conception or weddings – or perhaps both!

Dragon Fortunately, the Ox is a sound and realistic person who is unlikely to take unnecessary risks. For that reason, the financial pitfalls which lie ahead in the Dragon year to trap the unwary do not pose the problem that they may do for those who are less astute. But it is never a fault to be careful.

Snake A very favourable period, with possible financial benefits from carefully maintained investments. If there have been disputes or legal problems, these have a greater chance of being resolved to your satisfaction. A good year for research, and for making new contacts.

Horse This is a period of seeming stagnation. Seed has to remain in the ground for quite a while before the grain can be harvested. Everything needs a period of rest; matters are waiting to happen. Make sure you don't mistake the leafless trees of winter for dead ones.

Sheep This would not be a favourable period for striking out in a new direction, or dealing with strangers. There are a number of obstacles ahead, and you should not underestimate the competition. But, after this difficult period is over, life begins to improve.

Monkey At last, there are signs that matters are going to go your way. Although there may be only slight improvements to start with, they are enough to spur you on to greater efforts. Use humour and surprise to turn events in your favour.

Rooster A successful year to come, particularly in the matter of personal relationships. But career advancement is also indicated, and also perhaps official recognition of your achievements in the form of a certificate, medal, or election to some prestigious organization.

Dog Problems this year are likely to result in disruption in your home. Make sure that adverse circumstances are not forced on you.

Pig This is generally a period of quiet improvement. Finances are sound, and home life is tranquil. There is certainly a greater feeling of satisfaction with your circumstances. The Pig month (November) is a good time to decorate your home.

OTHER ANIMAL INFLUENCES

How the other animal signs in the horoscope chart influence the Ox

Rat Adds balance to the Ox and increases forward-thinking potential. It adds flexibility to what could be an obstinate nature.

Ox An extra Ox increases staying power. This could heighten a dislike of change, which could be put to use if there is an interest in real estate.

Tiger This reveals internal conflict and a feeling that life has more to offer. One side wants to thrust ahead and the other wishes to stay put.

Rabbit A favourable sign which reveals a need for close family ties. Happiness is found in a rural environment.

Dragon A sign of danger flickers. It is important to follow one's better judgement, and avoid a tendency to take risks.

Discretion and experience is the best course of action.

Snake A very favourable sign of business acumen, signifying wealth and success through the sale of land or property. It gives insight, and enables the Ox to plan ahead with foresight.

Horse (Flower of Love) It is difficult to ride two horses at once. Here, this means problems in relationships occur when one is torn between two partners.

Sheep Dangers may arise from inner conflict and indecisiveness. There is a feeling that not enough is being done, and a dissatisfaction with life generally. It is important to accept your own true nature.

Monkey This Ox is gifted with technical ability and practical skills. There are favourable opportunities in matters dealing with works of art, or products of high-quality manufacture.

Rooster A very favourable sign, especially where commerce and trade are involved. It indicates an accumulation of wealth in later life, and a luxurious home filled with every comfort.

Dog Inner discontent results from dissatisfaction with home circumstances, revealed by a constant urge to change your surroundings, and a lack of will to change the location. Firm decisions are needed.

Pig (Post Horse) Stress results from a need to travel, though the real wish is to retain your roots. It is difficult to have to live in two places at once, and the strain can be a burden.

THE TIGER

HOUSE: *Development*
BRANCH: III / *Yang*
ELEMENT: *Wood*

For the Chinese, the king of the animals is not the lion, but the tiger. As proof of this, the stripes on a tiger's head form the Chinese character **Wang** *meaning 'king'. It follows, that, years ago, when the branches were replaced by animal names, the tiger was the obvious choice for an animal to represent the first month of the Chinese year, even though this is not the first sign of the Chinese zodiac. The beginning of spring, rather than the depths of winter, is more appropriate for royalty. Thus, the Tiger represents authority, government and judgement (the Queen of England, not surprisingly, is a Tiger), and symbolizes luxury, power and discipline, the ruling classes and uniformed services.*

PERSONALITY

For the Tiger personality, 'magnetism' is the key word. It would be difficult for the Tiger to be a spy, other than one of the James Bond variety, since merging unnoticed into the background would be an almost impossible task! The Tiger needs attention, and in any group of people will always stand out – if not through fashionable and expensive finery, then through sheer physical presence. The Tiger takes command naturally, assuming that everyone around is there to follow orders. However, when this self-assertiveness is misinterpreted – or recognized – as aggressiveness, it is often a cause for offence. Such a trait might be admired in some men, but in a woman it can be a cause for scorn. 'Never bring a Tigress into the house' is a saying of the Chinese, who maintain a traditional idea of the role of women in society.

COMPATIBILITY

How people born in the year of the Tiger relate to people born in the different animal years

Rat This can be an easy-going relationship, provided both partners recognize that the other does not always have the same interests. The Rat should not expect the Tiger to sacrifice interests outside the home. There are so many opportunities for sharing experiences that occasionally they can go their separate ways.

Ox A Chinese proverb states that 'One Ox can fight two Tigers', suggesting that this can be an uneasy relationship. The Tiger needs to take a subordinate role for a change and learn to adapt and to smile resignedly – or life will be uncomfortable.

Tiger A strangely unpredictable relationship where two very similar individuals – who ought to delight in their mutual interests – act as rivals. There is no middle ground – both are rulers of their own kingdoms. They must learn to be at peace, or there will be war.

Rabbit This is a remarkably satisfactory partnership. Though their methods may oppose one another, they have their own ways of solving problems, and both are astute enough to realize that the other has good reasons for following their chosen course of action. They also make a particularly successful business partnership.

Dragon Whether in business or romance, this partnership is wildly successful, but not necessarily enduring. It is ideal for an intense, passionate fling, but in a long-term relationship the constant need for magic and surprise may begin to pall after a while.

Snake An element of mistrust lingers – each partner wants to be able to read the other's mind. They are concerned lest the other has a secret, or perhaps has discovered one but is not saying. In a business partnership, however, the Snake can have a productive and important role to play in the smooth management of the business.

Horse This is one of the best partnerships that the Tiger can choose. What the Tiger values most in the Horse is understanding, loyalty and support. Whether male or female, the Horse partner would be supportive and a good listener when the Tiger is beset with problems.

Sheep Although the Tiger may consider the Sheep unadventurous, that is why the Tiger needs the Sheep. Sometimes a reliable and restful change from the cut and thrust of everyday life is exactly what is needed. Life can have too much excitement. Harmony and placidity are not to be underrated.

Monkey It may have been a frisson of danger that brought these two together, for this partnership seems to have an unconventional undercurrent. Both must adjust their personalities to match the other's qualities if the relationship is to survive. In a business setting, a third member should be added to the team to bind it amicably.

Rooster Two highly charged individuals with their own brand of energetic vitality. Respect between them is not enough – there has to be admiration too. If they are going to do something together, it should be to the advantage of both, and for the right reasons. When one partner is visually attractive, jealousy can be a problem.

Dog This is the second of the Tiger's most favourable relationships. They respect each other's ideals, and are pleased, at last, to find that their high principles are not scoffed at or considered old-fashioned. There is tremendous support both in the home and at work, and an eagerness to share the partner's problems as well as their successes.

Pig In this relationship there are distinct lines drawn between responsibilities as breadwinner and homemaker, and little interest taken in the other's domestic or career problems. Romantically, there are likely to be collisions. In business it is better when these two have separate roles.

35

FAVOURABLE AND UNFAVOURABLE PERIODS

How the Tiger fares in periods ruled by the different animal signs

Rat This is a favourable time for the Tiger, with the possibility of long-distance travel combining business with leisure. The financial position of Tiger types is improved, especially concerning long-term investments.

Ox A difficult transition period, fraught with disputes and unexpected obstacles, although the stoppages are really only postponements. Prepare for all eventualities.

Tiger An energetic period for the Tiger, bringing personal success and the accomplishment of short-term objectives. Those looking for promotion should not be afraid to put their names forward.

Rabbit There is great pleasure during this period in observing the success of loved ones. Family achievements at this time bring a feeling of fulfilment to you. This is also a favourable time for marriage arrangements and related matters.

Dragon A good sign for pleasant surprises. The Dragon is a bringer of luck for most people, especially the Tiger. But let the luck come to you – don't make rash speculations.

Snake Not one of the most favourable signs for the Tiger. Beware of malice, for sometimes words hurt more than stones. But if the Monkey and Pig are also present together, then there is good fortune.

Horse One of the Tiger's two most favourable signs. The benefits are not confined to financial stability, but are also evident in the quality of life. Progress can be made in relationships where rivalries have caused problems in the past.

Sheep For the Tiger, this is an indifferent time. There may be family problems in which you have to assert some kind of authority, though your interference may be resented. But it is better to speak your mind.

Monkey During Monkey periods there is a need for caution, as Monkeys have the knack of being able to catch the Tiger by the tail. If the Snake is present, domestic affairs need to be seen to; if the Pig features, legal matters could be troublesome.

Rooster A turbulent period of great change. There will be confrontations with rivals, but after a stormy session matters will be resolved to your satisfaction. Your leisure plans are likely to be disrupted.

Dog The second of the Tiger's most favourable signs. It brings auspicious influences to bear on any matters connected with the home (the building itself, rather than the people living there).

Pig The Pig, unfavourably positioned with regards to the Tiger, suggests domestic disputes over trivial matters are likely to arise. This is not likely to bother you, but other family members, unknown to you, may be upset.

OTHER ANIMAL INFLUENCES

How the other animal signs in the horoscope chart influence the Tiger

Rat Travel broadens the mind, as Water Tigers know well. They are constantly on the move, or planning other people's movements for them. Restless, they cannot settle unless they have a travel guide close at hand.

Ox When the Ox and Tiger conflict, the Ox is the winner. Inner stress can cause a fluctuating temperament. It is helpful to learn patience and study the sayings of Confucius.

Tiger Self-assurance is not a fault, but exaggerated self-esteem is. It is good to be ambitious, for otherwise there would be nothing to look forward to, but failure can be depressing.

Rabbit (Flower of Love) The most creative of Tiger types, the extra Wood in this Tiger's horoscope combines creativity with determination. They make fine artists, but sometimes their creativity is directed more towards releasing the creativity in others, through inspired teaching.

Dragon A favourable sign for the Tiger, producing the determination to enjoy the luxuries of life. Such a person may advance themselves to a high social position.

Snake This Fire sign provides intellectual stimulation, and a love of mathematical puzzles and enigmas. Tempers flare up easily, so it is best not to disturb this Tiger during periods of concentration.

Horse A very favourable input, increasing the Tiger's social outlook. It helps to make the very original Tiger more sociable. A good team leader.

Sheep A difficult sign, normally neutral in influence, but which may have a special force when combined with other animal signs. The horoscope needs to be studied in depth.

Monkey (Post Horse) A troublesome sign for the Tiger, which could indicate emigration or travel through business or family commitments to a place far from home.

Rooster Competition provides stimulation for these Tiger types. They are also skilled in handling accounts, whether their own or other people's. In business and social life, they achieve esteem and recognition.

Dog Perseverance is the keynote of this most practical person. The presence of the Earth element shows that great pride is taken in the home – easily distinguished from its neighbours by a highly characteristic style. Do not argue with this Dog–Tiger person, as your views are likely to be changed.

Pig On its own, the Pig in the Tiger's horoscope reveals mild irritation with domestic arrangements. There may be a constant need for change, and an underlying restlessness which can be disconcerting for those around you.

THE RABBIT

HOUSE: *Development*

BRANCH: **IV** / *Yin*

ELEMENT: *Wood*

The fourth sign of the Chinese zodiac rules the month which includes the spring equinox, when the days begin to lengthen. Similarly, it rules the time between 5 and 7 am – when night gives way to day. It is symbolic of new life, and applies to all matters connected with children, their care, education and creation. Because the Rabbit is a universal symbol for spring, it was an obvious choice for the fourth sign.

The ancient symbol for the fourth sign was a drawing of a group of stars, the Pleiades, which could be seen on the horizon when spring approached. Also, because medicinal herbs are best when they are freshly collected at dawn, the sign of the Rabbit is associated with the healing arts.

PERSONALITY

Belonging to the same house as the Tiger – Development – the Rabbit conquers, but by diplomacy rather than outward aggression. But, as the Tiger's yin counterpart, the Rabbit displays strong defensive qualities when trouble threatens those dear to its heart.

Usually, however, the Rabbit wears an air of kind tranquillity and tender compassion, in which people are ready to confide. People whose year animal is the Rabbit are endowed with a caring personality, usually yearning for large families and, if deprived of the joy of their own offspring, are likely to enter those professions involved in children's education, nursing, looking after the underprivileged, or even animal welfare. Rabbit personalities are gifted judges of character, valuing sincerity and despising deception.

COMPATIBILITY

How people born in the year of the Rabbit relate to people born in the different animal years

Rat The Rabbit fares better than the Rat in this relationship. The element of the Rat is Water, which nourishes the Rabbit's element – Wood. Although the Rabbit may feel that this partnership has managed to balance responsibilities, the Rat may harbour a secret resentment – perhaps unjustified – which can lead to uncomfortable situations.

Ox There is romance and passion here. These two personalities can happily live alongside each other, sharing when they need to, or affecting indifference when they perceive the other's need to have time alone. Generally, the partnership progresses steadily and satisfactorily, but there are occasional unexpected flashes of enjoyment adding zest to life.

Tiger The yang side of the coin, the Tiger can bring excitement and even luxury to the Rabbit's life. Meeting with the Tiger would mean a disruption in domestic life, and a widening of the social circle. New ideas lead to adventures which could never have been considered in earlier days. On the other hand, the Tiger welcomes the Rabbit's steadying influence.

Rabbit It will seem that these two have known each other all their lives. Their interests and ambitions are very close, and even memories of times before they met will have many common incidents. A happy couple who, nevertheless, may have open opinions regarding their commitments to each other.

Dragon Astrologically, this is not the best choice of partner. The Dragon may have presented an aura of exoticism and excitement at first, but the initial impression may begin to tarnish quite rapidly. It is unlikely that there will be mutual support when circumstances force them to evaluate their financial commitments to each other.

Snake 'When the Rabbit meets the Snake, there is true happi-ness' runs an old Chinese proverb. Is it necessary to add to those delightful words of wisdom?

Horse Chinese astrologers do not consider this to be one of the more favourable relation-ships for the Rabbit. The Horse may seem concerned and car-ing, but sometimes this may be a way of seeking attention. Too many demands are put on the Rabbit, who may be expending energy on emotional support that might be more profitably diverted to the more deserving.

Sheep One of the Rabbit's two ideal partnerships. These two have much in common and can develop a partnership which brings a peaceful home life and a stable business relationship. There is almost a telepathic rap-port between them.

Monkey How long will the Rabbit tolerate the Monkey's antics? Patience is not merely a virtue in this stormy setting, but a necessary quality. There are so many differences in lifestyle and attitude that there are bound to be disputes. Both partners have something to offer the other – though at some cost.

Rooster Something drew these two together. In time, however, the Rabbit may find the Rooster too full of self-esteem, while the Rooster may come to consider the Rabbit aloof. They both need to see things from the other's point of view.

Dog This partnership works better when the Dog is the older partner, and perhaps the bread-winner. Otherwise, there may be an imbalance, which can lead to feelings of discontent. They may stay together without realizing that, instead of being a partner-ship, they are two individuals.

Pig Another satisfying relation-ship for the Rabbit personality. Both partners share a love of home and family. Whatever the circumstances, they will lead a comfortable life. Their content-ment allows them to apply themselves to their business free from worry.

FAVOURABLE AND UNFAVOURABLE PERIODS

How the Rabbit fares in periods ruled by the different animal signs

Rat On the surface, this is a difficult phase with several problems. But resources are available to tackle the difficulties. Nevertheless, life would be easier without these hindrances.

Ox A favourable period, bringing benefits from sources that may have been forgotten. There is a greater sense of security. A change of circumstance brings the answer to a problem which has been a source of worry.

Tiger A hectic period in which it is possible to achieve great success, provided you make the effort to apply yourself to the task in hand. It reveals rewards for one's own efforts, rather than unexpected good fortune.

Rabbit All matters of the heart are favourable at this time. It is a good period for romance, getting engaged, marriage or raising children. Creative artists will be inspired. All matters to do with agriculture or gardening will bring satisfaction.

Dragon A period when it is dangerous to take risks or speculate. It is not a favourable time for taking part in public performances, or giving speeches and presentations. If this is unavoidable, great attention to every detail is vitally important.

Snake A favourable period for all matters concerning accounts, finance and legal matters. Days marked by the Snake sign are favourable for romantic liaisons or arranging weddings.

Horse There are likely to be obstacles put in your way by a critical and negative colleague. The reasons are likely to be jealousy or resentment. Although the interference may be unpleasantly intrusive, it is unlikely to develop.

Sheep A highly potent period for pressing ahead with your main objectives. Finalize your plans, and act on them. Do not let opportunities escape by being too hesitant.

Monkey Your working environment is likely to be marred by a period of petty annoyances, especially where equipment is concerned. Technical problems can be resolved eventually.

Rooster A transitional period, seeing the end of one phase and the possibility to embark on another. Not the most positive time, so observe caution in any personal relationship or business dealing for which there are grounds to be suspicious.

Dog If it is possible to postpone any important decisions, it would be best to do so. Indeed, a plan which you were hoping to complete may fall through, though it would not have been a success had you continued.

Pig A positive period, allowing you to spend time – and money – on making your environment more comfortable. Follow any leads which attract you as this is a period of personal development and life improvement.

OTHER ANIMAL INFLUENCES

How the other animal signs in the horoscope chart influence the Rabbit

Rat (Flower of Love) There are indications of more than one spouse or a romantic affair while married. The complications which result from this will lead to financial depredations.

Ox This sign provides support through difficult periods, and shows recovery from illness. There is also a capacity for hard work, which is greatly admired.

Tiger A favourable sign showing that help may come from someone in authority. Some problems can be solved more easily than had been anticipated, once the right connections are made.

Rabbit The doubled year animal here shows increased self-awareness, and an ability to work independently despite a lack of encouragement from those who should help.

Dragon An unfavourable combination, which suggests financial instability. It is important to handle the cashflow carefully, and budget for emergencies.

Snake (Post Horse) This is a very favourable sign, bringing great happiness. A partnership with someone from abroad is a strong possibility. Children may be born overseas.

Horse There is a difficult inner personality clash, wanting to be an individual, and yet desperate for social attention. It is important to live in a situation where there are people who can respect your need to be alone sometimes.

Sheep The friendly and caring nature of the Rabbit personality, plus the romantic outlook and the desire to help others, is magnified in this happy combination of signs.

Monkey This personality is outwardly respectable and career-orientated, but has an inner mischievous streak which can lead to embarrassing situations. Harness the rebellious nature positively by learning some practical technique or craft.

Rooster An unruly sign, which can pose a warning if either the Rat or the Horse is also present in the horoscope. Such people are liable to be misunderstood, which makes them appear to be irrational, since they are afraid to voice their inner anxieties. Be more open.

Dog There is a strongly defensive nature in this character, both with regards to your family and your home. Kindly advice may be resented and mistaken for implied criticism.

Pig A dedicated worker, who will make every effort to ensure that the family have all possible home comforts. A very favourable combination.

THE DRAGON

龍

HOUSE: *Spirituality*

BRANCH: *V / Yang*

ELEMENT: *Earth*

There is a huge difference between Eastern and Western concepts of the Dragon. For both cultures, the Dragon is an ancient and grotesque beast with supernatural powers. But, whereas in the West it is a fire-breathing monster, in China its power may be benign and it can bring wealth, honour and fame. In evolutionary terms it is seen as the pinnacle – the humblest creature aspires to its ultimate metamorphosis. In the human world, the emperor himself sits on the Dragon throne.

In Chinese astronomy the Dragon constellation occupies a whole 'quarter' of the sky, being associated with the East and the spring rains. The only mythical animal of the twelve, the Dragon is the symbol of magic and the supernatural.

PERSONALITY

People born under the sign of the Dragon are influenced by its heady magnificence. This stimulates the outgoing extrovert side of the personality and, when too powerful, leads to rashness, illogical reasoning and reckless speculation. Such people are drawn to the exotic and the unknown. Life is a either a joy or a tragedy, to be experienced to the full. Small wonder that such people are often drawn to careers in the theatre, which itself is a form of magical experience. The careers which suit the Dragon are those which involve transformation, grand gestures and presentation to an admiring audience.

Flamboyance and exuberance are hard to hide, but one aspect which needs to be carefully controlled is the Dragon's tendency to take risks and gamble: nothing could be more dangerous than a handsome win, as a lifetime may be spent trying to repeat it.

COMPATIBILITY

How people born in the year of the Dragon relate to people born in the different animal years

Rat Whether in business or romance, the Rat could be the ideal companion for the Dragon. They make a handsome couple, and find much to admire in each other. The Rat could play a useful role helping the Dragon to manage its finances, but may also be a source of inspiration for the Dragon's adventurous schemes.

Ox An Earth element sign, the Ox tends to restrain the Dragon, keeping it under control. While this may be good for the partnership, it may make the Dragon partner feel imprisoned, leading to resentment, which may damage the relationship in time.

Tiger Two soulmates who share a love of excitement, high society and the good things in life. For them, it may be a breathtaking relationship, but the danger is that fanning the flames may make the fires burn out only too soon. Friends can only look on and shake their heads.

Rabbit A Chinese proverb says 'When the Rabbit appears, the Dragon's fortune disappears', thus warning against this partnership. Circumstances they cannot understand may douse the fire of excitement that brought these two people together.

Dragon Two partners of the same sign usually bond together amicably, but the Dragon is an exception. It is such a compelling sign that two together can be overpowering. There could be too much personal rivalry standing in the way of true compatibility.

Snake The Snake and Dragon are partners in the House of Spirituality. An intriguing couple, each with enough individuality to bring stimulation and freshness into the relationship, and with so many shared interests that they have no difficulty in relating to each other. A close bond of kinship ensures a stable partnership.

Horse There may be fewer points of contact in this relationship than might be seen in some more obviously ideal partnerships, but an underlying magnetism has drawn these two people together. Their differences are clear enough, and that is the way they prefer it.

Sheep These two may find life together exasperating at times. While each may feel the other has praiseworthy qualities, there is often a wish that these might be evident more often, and the more irritating characteristics occasionally kept under wraps. Don't be afraid to risk hurting the other's feelings, and speak frankly about your concerns.

Monkey A wonderfully bizarre harmony exists between these two exotic personalities. Romantically, and in business, their ideas and shared enthusiasm is so energetic that by combining forces they can achieve enormous success in a business venture, provided that it is sufficiently extraordinary.

Rooster These two are sufficiently independent to be able to lead separate lives, and yet live together amicably as a couple. It is a relationship which suits them perfectly, but other couples would not be able to sustain such a precarious partnership. They may walk on a knife edge, but they are sure-footed.

Dog Astrologically, this is not the ideal partnership for either the Dog or the Dragon. The Dog character is basically down-to-earth and traditional, whereas the Dragon is just the opposite. Some other force must bind them together, and this is the fact that their own 'inner element', Yang Earth, is identical.

Pig These two personalities have different priorities, and one's outlook on life may not match the other partner's views. Individual characteristics may be an irritation to the other, and a cause of upset. But, if there were no love between these two, they could not stay together. They would rather tolerate a situation which can't be changed than leave it.

FAVOURABLE AND UNFAVOURABLE PERIODS

How the Dragon fares in periods ruled by the different animal signs

Rat Periods ruled by the Rat are the most favourable times for the Dragon where financial matters are concerned. However, it is important to handle the budget wisely, as these good phases are not permanent.

Ox It will be difficult to make changes during this stagnant period. Don't become frustrated by obstacles, but instead plan what your next move can be when the opportunity arises.

Tiger There is potential for career improvement, and recognition for successful achievement of your objectives. The greater the effort made during this fruitful phase, the more welcome will be the rewards.

Rabbit It is best not to put too much reliance on the successful outcome of any project which is planned to come to an end during a Rabbit period. Unexpected demands on both time and finances are likely to cause troublesome delays.

Dragon Do not allow overconfidence to lead you to rashness during this auspicious period. Although there are some very favourable trends, with the promise of rich rewards, it is easy to become caught up, and exaggerate their potential benefits.

Snake This is a period when you are likely to benefit from projects that have already been under way, but not so favourable for beginning long-term ventures. A confident phase, which shows success resulting from carefully planned moves.

Horse This period is very favourable for socializing, teamwork, or arranging events involving many people. This time also favours sporting events, male activity, and outdoor ventures. It is less favourable for matters more usually associated with women's interests.

Sheep This is not a phase recommended for starting work on new projects. It may be difficult

to enlist the help of people who would be vital to the successful completion of plans. It would be far better to use the time as a waiting period of consolidation, and redrafting plans.

Monkey A vibrant phase for the Dragon character, particularly ideal for any technical matters, such as the purchase or installation of new machinery. For longer time periods, it could be seen as an ideal opportunity to acquire new skills or embark on a career move.

Rooster In the short term, a woman in a senior position, or a person whose wishes you have to accept, is critical of your plans, and wishes to substitute his or her own ideas for yours. In the longer term, finances are likely to be diverted away from your objective.

Dog A difficult phase fraught with hindrances and obstacles, especially with regard to your residence. You may find it necessary to move house or undertake repairs – either of which rapidly eat up both your time and your financial resources.

Pig This time period is sufficiently distant from the Dragon for it to be neither a help nor a hindrance. Use the time for continuing processes already in motion, solving problems as they arise, and working steadily towards the goal that you have already set yourself.

OTHER ANIMAL INFLUENCES

How the other animal signs in the horoscope chart influence the Dragon

Rat This is a favourable sign to have in the Dragon's horoscope, indicating financial reward, creative ability and a flair for innovative business ventures.

Ox Here the Dragon's reckless streak is tempered with sound common sense. Emigration may be planned, but forestalled because of home commitments.

Tiger (Post Horse) This combination indicates long-distance commuting, or emigration. There will be a period of luxurious living, ideally late in life.

Rabbit This indicates problems with relatives. Great care must be taken in any financial dealings that involve members of the family, as it is difficult to be objective where close relatives are concerned.

Dragon Such a person may easily take to the stage. A very exuberant character who should take care not to antagonize business colleagues.

Snake The Snake reduces the extrovert qualities of the Dragon; but a love of the occult and the mystic arts is not reduced. Such people are often gifted with psychic prowess.

Horse This is a favourable influence, enhancing social skills and providing a steadying influence without constraining the Dragon's freedom of expression.

Sheep The Dragon's artistic leanings are directed more towards musical and social activities, often involving the family. Professional aspirations, however, may not be fulfilled.

Monkey If it were possible to enhance the Dragon's exuberant style, it would be revealed by the Monkey in the horoscope. Wit and cleverness are enhanced by technical practicality.

Rooster (Flower of Love) If the Dragon is a man, a weakness for the opposite sex may be his undoing; if a woman, jealous rivals can cause misery. Have no secrets from your partner.

Dog There are things that we want to do, and things that have to be done. In this case, life seems to be a constant battle between the two.

Pig Beneath the brash devil-may-care personality lies a calm, sensible and reasoned inner self striving to get out. Let the head rule the heart occasionally.

THE SNAKE

HOUSE: *Spirituality*
BRANCH: VI / *Yin*
ELEMENT: *Fire*

The Snake is the Dragon's yin counterpart in the House of Spirituality. One may assume that the reason why the Snake was chosen to symbolize the sixth sign was because of its similar appearance to a dragon, but this theory falls flat when you consider the contrasting pairs of animals in the other houses. The real reason lies in the shape of the 'pre-zodiac' sign. In ancient Chinese script it was written like a reverse '9', and described in the oldest Chinese dictionary 'as being curled like a snake'. The Snake symbolizes elegance through refinement and artistic restraint. According to a Chinese proverb, 'to draw a snake with legs' is to destroy the integrity of something that is already perfect by trying to make it even better.

PERSONALITY

The fundamental qualities of the Snake personality are summed up by the words 'mystical' and 'minimalist'. The typical Snake characteristics are quiet superiority, a preference for listening rather than speaking, and an air of calculated indifference. A gift for languages is common, while many Snake types have an intuitive flair which borders on the psychic. The Snake learns by remaining silent. Where secrets are concerned, the Snake is indefatigably acquisitive.

Snake people make good researchers, lawyers – even spies – because of their ability to seek out information which can be of use to them in the future, no matter how distant. Their methods are subtle, and they can merge invisibly into the background. In appearance, they are always elegant and smart, but never overdressed.

COMPATIBILITY

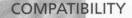

How people born in the year of the Snake relate to people born in the different animal years

Rat A Chinese proverb says 'The Snake eats the Rat.' The attraction between them may be very strong, but it is clear that the Snake takes the lead. It is important for the Snake to understand the Rat's need to be an individual. There may be matters which have been left unsaid for fear of causing hurt.

Ox Outwardly, no two creatures could be more different than the lumbering Ox and the nimble Snake. But in human terms, there is a powerful force which cements the bond between the practical earthiness of the Ox and the mystical glamour of the Snake. One of the two 'perfect' relationships for the Snake.

Tiger No doubt these two have differences of opinion on most matters, though it was through their similar social circles that they met. Perhaps both were looking to the other for like-minded companionship, only to find later that their interests were not all that similar. A relationship which needs careful nurturing.

Rabbit 'When the Rabbit meets the Snake, there is true happiness', runs a Chinese proverb. Although this is not one of the two 'perfect' relationships for the Snake, tradition says that the love between these two transcends barriers. They must not let mutual attraction blind them to the realities of everyday life.

Dragon The reverse side of the coin, the Dragon tends to take more out of the relationship than it puts in. The Snake bears no resentment, however, feeling happy to be part of a close-knit partnership. There may be difficulties when the Snake counts the hidden costs of this liaison.

Snake For romantic liaisons, there is a gentle mutual understanding between two Snake partners. Trouble may occur in a business partnership, same-sex friendship, or between family members of the same Snake sign. The one unfavourable aspect of

the Snake's temperament then surfaces: its interference – usually born of rivalry or jealousy.

Horse At first, this seems an everyday kind of relationship. If the ages are a year apart then the element of the Snake's year supports that of the Horse, and so helps to consolidate their partnership. But when the gap is wider, their rapport may not be as strong, as both will need to express their feelings differently.

Sheep This is a happy relationship where two individuals from different walks of life find that they have much to share. This has all the ingredients for a loving, supportive partnership, and a comfortable home life. Both will endeavour to make their partner secure and free from anxiety. Troubles will rarely last long, and storms are weathered with fortitude.

Monkey There is a likelihood of friction between these two. Their views on life are remarkably different, and it is sometimes a wonder how they got

together in the first place. It is not so much their shared interests as their disagreements which keep this couple together.

Rooster This is the second of the two 'perfect' relationships for the Snake. There is strong mutual admiration and respect for each other. The partnership should go further than a romantic attachment, for their combined talents could bring them success in the commercial world.

Dog Their worlds are far apart. Even if they are from the same stock, this is more a partnership of deference and respect than one of equals. It is important to share, discuss matters together, and not take the other's opinions for granted.

Pig These two try to please each other, yet never manage to discover what the other really wants. Sometimes life can be exasperating: in trying to help, the situation is only made worse. Get back to basics, and don't be afraid to mention trivial things which are actually important.

FAVOURABLE AND UNFAVOURABLE PERIODS

How the Snake fares in periods ruled by the different animal signs

Rat This is a period of aggressive acquisition. You can achieve success – but only by making the effort to thrust yourself forward, perhaps at the expense of losing friends in the process. Consider the options.

Ox Hard work repays handsomely: a very favourable, happy period where dedicated commitment to your goals brings rewards which have long-lasting benefits.

Tiger This is a period beset by problems. In legal matters, take the easy option – fighting for your rights may bring a hollow victory. Withdraw gracefully, and return to the fray later.

Rabbit The emphasis during this period is on personal happiness. All other considerations – whether financial, career, or even health, are given lower priority and laid to one side. Enjoy the opportunities that life brings before they pass you by irredeemably.

Dragon The rice doesn't gather itself. This is a positive phase, provided that you are willing to exert yourself and reap the harvest. If you are planning to take a new direction in life, this could be the right moment.

Snake This phase is ideal for closing one chapter and opening a new one. Your personal career and objectives come very much to the fore, and there will be opportunities for you to meet valuable new contacts.

Horse This is a period of continuation, but within a changed environment. Buildings may be altered, or the people around you will move on, though your own position continues as before.

Sheep You will be called to assist someone close to you, which may involve making a financial sacrifice, or there could be great demands made on your time. You should not resent this, however, as your first concern is the other person's welfare.

Monkey This is an unfavourable period for investing in new machinery, whether for business or the home. It is worthwhile checking that you have adequate insurance to cover mechanical breakdowns.

Rooster A very favourable phase. You should take advantage of the revitalizing energy to make some useful changes to your life. If you have been planning a 'once-in-a-lifetime' holiday, take it now.

Dog You should concentrate on the home front for the moment. There may be reasons for considering your location and what might be done to improve your living arrangements.

Pig Disruption to family life is likely – relatives who visit may outstay their welcome. Offering a friend the use of the spare room for a short while may be taken as an invitation to move in. Be careful how you phrase your offers of help.

OTHER ANIMAL INFLUENCES

How the other animal signs in the horoscope chart influence the Snake

Rat Financial obstacles are usually more of a nuisance than a serious problem in this instance. There may never be as much as you would like in the bank, but there will always be enough to live on.

Ox There is inner strength in the Ox which, added to the Snake's intelligence, makes a capable and practical worker with management and leadership capabilities.

Tiger The normally retiring Snake personality is given more physical presence and assertiveness by the authoritative qualities of the inner Tiger. However, this tends to shorten patience, and an explosive temperament may result.

Rabbit There is great satisfaction to be had in personal success and achievement. Romantic partnerships are very intense, but outside the intimate circle there is little need for further social contact.

Dragon Here considerable self-confidence and a somewhat superior demeanour produce a reluctance to relate to those of a supposed lower social position. There is active interest in matters pertaining to the supernatural or unexplained.

Snake The typical characteristics of the Snake personality are enhanced, giving you the ability to analyse current trends, financial movements and even personality with uncanny accuracy – skills which can be used to personal advantage.

Horse (Flower of Love) The normally introspective quality of the Snake is balanced by the sociable character of the Horse, making this one of the more popular Snake personalities.

Sheep Cultural refinement and a love of the arts, in particular music, is suggested by this pair of zodiac signs. Family ties are strong, and the quality of life more than comfortable.

Monkey Although gifted with an artist's eye, and some manual dexterity, there may be frustration at not being able to put ideas into practice. But after a struggle the results are often successful.

Rooster An inner extrovert is trying to escape the constraints of the outwardly introvert. Once this Snake has sloughed its skin, personal satisfaction results.

Dog Life seems to have much more to offer, if only it were possible to get away from a difficult situation. Either move away or make the best of what you have.

Pig (Post Horse) Use your imagination to create a better environment for yourself and your family. If you can't cope on your own, don't be afraid to ask others for help. There are many who will be happy to assist, if you can summon the courage to admit that you need them.

THE HORSE

HOUSE: *Sexuality*
BRANCH: VII / *Yang*
ELEMENT: *Fire*

The ancient sign for the midday hour and the month containing the longest day of the year – both Horse periods – depicted a pair of scales to signify the midpoint between the first and second halves of the day or year.

The Horse belongs to the House of Sexuality, and rules over all matters concerning the division of the sexes, the allocation of their responsibilities and their mutual bonding. The Horse occupies a vital time position in the horoscope, and signifies when a particular set of circumstances reach their peak. Thus, if the Horse represents success and satisfaction with life, it should ideally be found in later years.

PERSONALITY

The influence of the seventh sign heightens the need for social relationships. Its original connection with outdoor life signifies a leaning towards team sports. The typical Horse follows the latest trends and wants to be first to hear and relay news. Their opinions are strong, but usually predictable.

While the typical Horse male follows the old Chinese notion that the woman's place is in the home, the Horse female is the opposite. She is not so much an advocate of equal rights, as a believer in women's natural superiority. The Chinese traditionally fear women born in the year of the Horse, for they tend to be assertive and display authority. This is especially the case for women born in Fire Horse years (the last was 1966; the next, 2026). It was formerly the case that female babies born in those fateful years would be exposed to die, rather than growing to be dreaded Fire Horse women.

COMPATIBILITY

How people born in the year of the Horse relate to people born in the different animal years

Rat It would be very difficult to imagine two people with such opposing opinions. There is always a clash between the conventional and the innovative. Their relationship will succeed only if they can both have free rein to create the environment of their choice.

Ox It is said that the Ox and Horse never share the same stable. Although they do not share the same outlook on life, their views are so different that they don't bother to argue. Usually the Ox brings some stability into this relationship, and stops the Horse from galloping off.

Tiger This is the soulmate for the Horse. They have common ideals and, though they may approach their goals in different ways, they work together in harmony. In business and love, there is mutual respect which matures into affection. A successful and happy relationship.

Rabbit Sometimes family commitments have to take priority over social engagements and business. Without an understanding partner to help in the division of responsibilities, life can be difficult. It does not further family harmony when the Horse puts principle before what is mutually beneficial.

Dragon This can be an exciting relationship if both partners remember occasionally that they live on planet Earth. Dreams and ambitions can sometimes be realized, and the most extravagant objectives may sometimes become reality. But there come times when it is vital to deal with the ordinary humdrum affairs of everyday life as well.

Snake Social or business contact may have brought these two together, and it seemed to make sense. But there is more to life than following what is the most practical or convenient path. Look more carefully into ways in which you and your partner can widen your experiences and look to new horizons.

Horse Two Horse types can live together happily, and share many fulfilling moments. There are bound to be differences of opinion, but these will not intrude on their personal relationship, and are not important enough to quarrel over. Each respects the other's rights.

Sheep These two people believe in each other, and have a sincere bond of affection which is more than a romantic attachment. There is a great warmth and understanding which comes from within. Although one partner may be obliged to spend lengthy periods away from the home, separation is always a hardship for both of them.

Monkey The Chinese used to keep their horses amused by placing a monkey in the stable. In a relationship, the Monkey person is a stimulating companion, ever eager to share the latest gossip, information on the newest trends, and, in a business partnership, to uncover information regarding competitors and rival concerns.

Rooster The Horse personality finds many things to admire in the Rooster, but may find this partner has an attitude that is not wholly acceptable. Although there is much to be gained from this relationship, the Horse should not be afraid of hurting the Rooster's feelings when the situation becomes irksome.

Dog This is one of the two ideal relationships for the Horse, and it works well both in business and romance. They have similar ambitions, which are designed to increase their quality of life, but they are also able to pool their ideas so that their objectives can be realized. A happy couple who can look forward to prosperity.

Pig This is a comfortable partnership, and in many ways a traditional and conventional one. Often, these two will have independent means and different careers. Being separated on occasion does not trouble them unduly. When together again, they have no problem picking up where they left off.

FAVOURABLE AND UNFAVOURABLE PERIODS

How the Horse fares in periods ruled by the different animal signs

Rat This is not one of the most favourable periods; it should not be chosen as a period for targeting new ventures. It is worth remembering that this stagnant period is only temporary.

Ox If there are long-term plans to be drawn up, or large-scale commitments to be organized, this is a suitable time. Careful consideration of future prospects is more important than action at the moment.

Tiger A highly productive and creative period when new ideas can be undertaken with confidence. For all matters – career, business and relationships – this time is very productive.

Rabbit There are likely to be minor hold-ups causing delays. An illness, or adverse weather conditions, may mean that important engagements have to be postponed. However, the key word is 'postponement' rather than cancellation. Be prepared for the need to be flexible.

Dragon A favourable time for short-term projects. Longer-term commitments will prosper to some degree. Social events, the promotion of business by unconventional means, or exotic holidays, will repay investment.

Snake A favourable period for activities to continue, not for changing direction. Let things take their own course. Don't squander finances continuing with projects which should have been dropped.

Horse A great time to embark on new ventures, and strike out in whatever direction takes your fancy. Follow your instincts.

Sheep Your efforts in the past should now start to repay your investment in work, physical activity, or even your intellectual effort. Although initial enthusiasm for your schemes may fade, your commitment is sound.

Monkey An active period when you can put your plans into action. Work quickly, and don't be afraid to call in extra resources if you have to. The sooner you get everything under way, the easier it will be. Delays may prove costly.

Rooster Not an ideal time for dealing with other people. You may be presented with so many ideas that your original plan is obscured. Break the ties, and begin afresh.

Dog A highly favourable phase during which you feel revitalized and able to take on any commitment. By all means push ahead, for you will find that your enthusiasm will be infectious, and other people will want to join in. Use the time purposefully and constructively.

Pig An unsatisfactory period for great changes. This is a slow-moving stable phase, ideal for thinking about what you ought to be doing in a few years' time. Changes made now will have to be re-examined later.

OTHER ANIMAL INFLUENCES

How the other animal signs in the horoscope chart influence the Horse

Rat This classic combination of yin and yang produces people who are so well balanced that they are virtually neutral; they may go to great pains to avoid being partisan, but are in danger of giving the impression that they are prone to sit on the fence. But it is vital to consider the other horoscope signs in this special case.

Ox The Ox gives stability to a personality which might be somewhat volatile. The ideal environment would be one away from the city. Careers involving land are suggested.

Tiger A very powerful authoritative combination producing people who can make careers for themselves in management. Leadership qualities suggest the uniformed professions.

Rabbit (Flower of Love) Look at the whole horoscope, since, badly aspected, this combination suggests problems with health. Alternatively, it might indicate a career in nursing or working with children. The Flowers of Love sign reveals a secret romantic relationship.

Dragon This is a 'lucky' horoscope, showing strokes of good fortune bringing unexpected financial gains. But any inclination to gamble should be steadfastly avoided.

Snake Both mental and physical prowess are combined here to produce someone with varied talents who may be likely to follow two different careers. Detective work is a possibility.

Horse The emphasis on gender suggests a brightly sociable person in public who, in private, is withdrawn and rather timid when it comes to dealing with the opposite sex.

Sheep Quietly constructive, this combination reveals fairness and judgement, and an interest both in the physical and intellectual sides of human activity.

Monkey (Post Horse) The outgoing and extrovert qualities of the Horse character are heightened by the capriciousness of the Monkey sign. Taking unnecessary risks is dangerous. the Post Horse indicates emigration or long-distance commuting.

Rooster A somewhat abrasive nature is added to the qualities of this horoscope. A desire to be popular can be misinterpreted as self-indulgence. Judge people carefully.

Dog The important qualities of loyalty, a sense of duty and responsibility add to the attractive characteristics of this popular character. Friendships are long-lasting and sincere.

Pig Traditional methods and old-fashioned standards are more important than following the latest trends or fashions. Gullibility and a lack of caution are the main weaknesses.

THE SHEEP

HOUSE: *Sexuality*
BRANCH: VIII / *Yin*
ELEMENT: *Earth*

The ancient character for the eighth sign was a plough, signifying that, although the midday hour had passed, it was still not time to finish work. But the animal adopted for this sign had nothing to do with ploughing, being chosen to represent the sign's astrological function as the feminine aspect of the House of Sexuality. Flocks of sheep are all female, so the Sheep represents yin, the feminine side of personality or activity. The yin influence also represents intellectual or gently receptive qualities, as opposed to the physical or aggressively active ones; the arts, rather than sports. The Chinese word for 'sheep' – which somewhat confusingly, is yang – also means 'goat', or even 'ram'.

PERSONALITY

The Sheep represents all matters pertaining to women's interests, caring qualities, a desire to help others, female beauty and attraction, seductiveness, humility and – more importantly – patience. Additionally, it shows interest in literature and the arts, particularly music, and activities which can be shared. In the home, it represents the achievement of family harmony, and the means to achieve this through skills in cookery and food preparation.

But, although the Sheep is basically a feminine sign, it is favourable to find it in the horoscope of a man, or a woman whose animal sign is a yang one. Confucius said that a man who was brave enough to face a tiger unarmed was not as useful as the man who preferred to take a weapon with him. Thus, even the most staunchly military general should have some 'yin' quality, or he could not possibly succeed in his task.

COMPATIBILITY

How people born in the year of the Sheep relate to people born in the different animal years

Rat Although these two individuals have shared interests, they also have quite different attitudes to life in general. The Sheep may well wish that their Rat partner could be more understanding with regard to domestic matters that should be discussed by both of them.

Ox It would be foolish for the Ox to dismiss the Sheep's views as inconsequential. A failure to come to terms with the Sheep as an individual may lead to resentment. The Sheep may look up to the Ox respectfully, but the respect has to be deserved.

Tiger The Tiger can be a stimulating, but exhausting, companion for the Sheep. The Tiger partner has much to offer, however, in terms of companionship, security and financial support as well. But the Tiger, with its own principles and priorities, may expect the Sheep to conform too rigidly to these high ideals.

Rabbit There is great happiness to be found for this couple, who share many similar interests and work together to make their lives happier. Such a partnership is ideal for those wishing to raise a large family. In a second marriage, where there are children of both marriages, the family will be happily unified.

Dragon While home life is contented enough, this relationship is often strained because of the erratic nature of their finances. It is important to make provision for times when money is tight. Occasionally, the Sheep may wish that the partner could be more helpful.

Snake Despite their separate lives – perhaps due to being from different backgrounds – these two lead a happy and productive life together. There is prosperity, a thriving business, and happiness at home. Despite their varied interests, there is mutual enjoyment both in the finer things of life and in the more humdrum everyday pleasures which lie closer to home.

Horse A well-ordered household, offering a secure environment with everything in its place. This is not just in the arrangements of material objects, but also in the way that life is regulated. There is no room for inexplicable moods and temperaments – everyone in this family knows what is expected of them, what their responsibilities are and, in turn, what their rewards and privileges will be.

Sheep A partnership that is bound to find contentment, no matter what obstacles may come their way. Good fortune or bad fortune, everything is taken as it comes. The happiness of the relationship is a matter for the couple to cultivate and cherish.

Monkey This is a practical relationship from which both partners can benefit. By being able to go their separate ways, this couple are able to stay together. Provided that they can both understand their differences, they will have little to argue about. A fresh and stimulating companionship.

Rooster The attraction of opposites is often very stimulating. They have a shared goal in life, but the ways by which they reach those goals are quite different. Career and home life are best kept separate. This partnership works far better on a romantic level: in a business partnership their different approaches could cause friction.

Dog Although there may be problems in their relationship, these usually stem from the fact that both are trying to reach the same result in different ways. It is worth remembering that surprises do not always have the intended effect. Discussion before taking unilateral decisions will help to keep this relationship on an even keel.

Pig A very happy relationship, regarded by Chinese astrologers as the ideal choice for those for whom romance, home life and family are a priority. In a business partnership, there is greater chance of success if the end product is concerned with family or home life.

FAVOURABLE AND UNFAVOURABLE PERIODS

How the Sheep fares in periods ruled by the different animal signs

Rat The beginning of a lengthy unproductive phase. An unsuitable period for embarking on long-term projects, but progress may be expected on short-term ventures. Stay on your present course, and use the time constructively to plan the next move.

Ox The middle of a rather unproductive period. Conserve resources, rather than trying to branch out in new directions, or losses could result. Be patient and wait a little while longer.

Tiger This period marks the end of an unsatisfactory phase. At last it will be possible to start thinking about the future. Use the time constructively, gathering your resources in readiness.

Rabbit A very satisfactory phase, when renewed resources and outside stimulation provide the impetus and encouragement for you to advance. Use this constructive period to move house, change career or to improve your domestic and social life.

Dragon There will be unexpected benefits during this time, but don't make the mistake of thinking these will be permanent. A Chinese proverb says, 'Do not wait for the drought to dig a well.' Channel your new resources against the time when they may suddenly dry up.

Snake You should be starting to feel the benefits of a constructive surge forward in your life. Your personal life has taken an unexpected turn, and it is necessary to come to terms with the changes it has brought. A new career may have some initial creases to be ironed out.

Horse A demanding time, but do not complain, as it is for your own future benefit. For those looking for new partners in their lives, this is a promising phase.

Sheep A particularly favourable period with many personal benefits to be gained. Your family situation improves, career prospects look promising, and there is promise of increased financial security. If you are planning to move, the East would be very productive.

Monkey There is much activity, but little to show for it. But, as frustrating as the hindrances may be, they are only temporary.

Rooster An exciting period, full of new experiences. You may have to budget for extra expenditure at this time, but the benefits will be worthwhile.

Dog Home life becomes the focus of attention during this period, and you may feel the need to change your address. It is not a period favourable for you personally, although it may benefit other members of the family. Consider the options carefully.

Pig A very happy period in all matters. If you have any plans, and are looking for a suitable time to put these into action, now is the moment.

OTHER ANIMAL INFLUENCES

How the other animal signs in the horoscope chart influence the Sheep

Rat (Flower of Love) The Rat adds analytical reasoning to the Sheep's intellectual processes. Neither's actions or words are taken at face value. But personal principles could be swept overboard as a result of a passionate attachment that leads to problems.

Ox Although stamina and perseverance are additional qualities present here, inner stress could be caused by an inability to balance home life with the demands of work or business.

Tiger The Tiger type brings a defensive quality to a normally placid nature, which might suddenly erupt in an uncharacteristic bout of anger. Such mood changes, however, are usually justified.

Rabbit The caring nature of the Rabbit type and a sympathy for the underprivileged is enhanced. There is a love of children and animals, and this may influence career choices.

Dragon There is a touch of recklessness in what is otherwise a stable and reliable personality. Sudden impulse may cause occasional impetuosity, which is later regretted.

Snake (Post Horse) A well-intentioned interest in other people's business can be construed as neighbourly concern, but is often mistaken for inquisitiveness. Be discreet in your observations, as you do not want to have to move house for the wrong reasons.

Horse This personality is able to see both sides of an argument, and give balanced opinions on matters of delicacy. Such a person is often asked for confidential advice.

Sheep A deep concern for the affairs of home and family life is very laudable, but there is more to life. Other avenues should be explored, but a desire to expand your horizons may be stifled through misplaced loyalty.

Monkey A wealth of unused talent and inner gifts is not given the opportunity to be developed in this character. It would be a pity, however, if a lack of resources meant that ambitions were left unfulfilled.

Rooster Despite leading a somewhat conventional lifestyle, there is a hidden depth of extraordinary artistic talent which, when properly nurtured, can flourish unexpectedly in later life.

Dog This combination shows a great independence of spirit, and an ability to cope in the face of adversity. When the force of circumstances creates a difficult situation, it is not necessary to seek outside help.

Pig An inner happiness in this personality exudes a quiet confidence that other people find comforting and reassuring. Such a person is a strong support for others in times of trouble.

THE MONKEY

猴

HOUSE: *Career*
BRANCH: IX / *Yang*
ELEMENT: *Metal*

Although the ninth sign of the Chinese zodiac is popularly called the Monkey, its original character meant 'stretching'. It represented the late afternoon, before sunset when men were still working in the fields. The men would 'stretch' themselves before tackling the final batch of work to be done. To indicate this, the Chinese script showed a leather hide being stretched out on a frame for tanning. This word has come to signify technical skill and engineering (skills which then seemed beyond human abilities). Its meaning can be extended to any kind of manual dexterity, as well as machinery and mechanical devices of all kinds. The clever monkey, with its agile fingers, was an ideal choice to represent these qualities.

PERSONALITY

When Monkey people do not seem to have a mechanical bent, or exhibit any sign of manual dexterity, the Monkey's agility is revealed in their ability to manipulate language and ideas. They are able to talk themselves out of tricky situations, but equally might – through their desire to make a plausible story even more convincing – get themselves entangled in an ever more complex web of confusion.

Monkey characters tend to be very resourceful in other ways too and are very capable of finding easier – if somewhat unconventional – solutions to everyday problems. Although undoubtedly gifted, they sometimes lack enough self-confidence to follow their ideas through to the final stage. In the right company, however, and with sufficient encouragement and additional expertise, they can become tremendously successful.

COMPATIBILITY

How people born in the year of the Monkey relate to people born in the different animal years

Rat Although they travel by different routes, these partners have the same end in sight. They have their own ways of tackling problems, but work well together to produce a solution. As friends, they have much in common. In romance, there is great physical attraction. In business, it is a stimulating partnership.

Ox The Ox tends to be critical of the Monkey's continual stream of activity, much of which seems purposeless. The Monkey may feel that more encouragement could be forthcoming, and regret their partner's lack of enthusiasm. But their steadying influence is often necessary.

Tiger The Monkey had better tread very carefully here, for (to quote from the Chinese), while it may be easy to tie a bell to the Tiger when it sleeps, it is not so easy to retrieve it once the Tiger is awake. A sound piece of advice which is worth bearing in mind should these two decide to make their partnership permanent.

Rabbit There are enough problems in life without taking on more. Both partners have worries of their own, and need someone to sort their lives out, which together they find very difficult to do. It is worth confiding in someone outside the relationship who might be able to advise them when things are going wrong.

Dragon Together, these two volatile personalities kindle a fire which is almost impossible to extinguish. They have so much to offer each other. Both are too aware of their own gifts to be overawed by the other's presence, but there is great respect.

Snake In this relationship the Monkey person can feel torn between the trivial and the important. Serious advice is often ignored because there are more exciting things to do. It is fatal to expect others to pick up the pieces when things go wrong. The Snake finds it

difficult to do more than give advice, but sometimes action is necessary, too.

Horse Lively and sociable, this couple enjoy each other's wit and company. Their relationship is based on trust and admiration. They will never travel far from each other, and yearn to be in touch. Happiness and success to both of them.

Sheep Usually, the attraction between these two develops gently after a friendly relationship. The admiration may have been from afar, and their mutual attraction may have taken them both by surprise. Though they may be materially close, in the sense that they come from the same backgrounds, they have quite different aspirations.

Monkey What a lively relationship this is likely to be! Their bonds may seem to be loosely tied, and in public they may not appear to be the most affectionate of couples, but the understanding between them lies very deep. A happy, hectic existence

lies ahead. Not everyone would envy their lifestyle, but their joy is unmistakable.

Rooster A very satisfying partnership, whether in a short-term affair, a lifetime commitment, or a business partnership. But it could never be an ordinary relationship. These two can make a tremendous success of whatever they want to achieve together.

Dog A mutually supportive partnership, with two like-minded individuals who can go their own independent ways when they wish, but who value their partner's companionship and support. Despite occasional differences, there is a strong bond of attachment between them, making occasional separation painful for both.

Pig Occasional arguments usually centre on domestic responsibilities. Different priorities lead to conflict. It is better to identify what each partner expects of the other and, when terms are agreed, these must be kept faithfully. They won't be, of course.

FAVOURABLE AND UNFAVOURABLE PERIODS

How the Monkey fares in periods ruled by the different animal signs

Rat This is a highly stimulating and creative period, which the Monkey can use constructively by embarking on a new departure in life. Whether for career advancement, financial improvement, stabilizing a relationship or moving house, this is a positive moment.

Ox A difficult phase. Problems must be dealt with as soon as they arise; otherwise they may become permanent obstacles that obstruct your advancement. It is not a suitable period for changing your place of work or residence.

Tiger It is best not to get into situations which may cause problems with authority. Do not take risks in your business, and ensure that papers and documents are in order. Faced with a confrontation by someone in a higher position, try to delay the interview.

Rabbit It is advisable not to exert yourself during this static phase. It may be necessary to postpone plans because of the unexpected ill-health of a member of your family. Use the period as a fallow time during which you can regain your strength in readiness for a new beginning.

Dragon This is a very favourable phase, when you are capable of achieving great personal success. It is also a timely moment to start afresh. Financial reward is also promised, but you budget your resources nevertheless. The extra benefits will be exhausted eventually.

Snake Be careful not to give away any personal information. Secrets inadvertently passed to another can cause harm. It is better not to let people take you into their confidence, as what you learn may not be to your advantage.

Horse This is a period of quiet confidence and inner satisfaction. Life should run both smoothly and satisfactorily. There are opportunities for meeting with new friends, and your social life – though quiet – will expand to draw in some very interesting people.

Sheep Use this quiet period for making plans. It may seem that very little is happening, but great changes are to be made, and you should be ready for them. Make an assessment of your present position, and what would have to be done if you suddenly had to leave.

Monkey This is a wonderful period for you to travel abroad – the north-east and south-east hold great prospects for you. Whether this is to follow your heart, or a business venture, the result will bring you joy and happiness.

Rooster You can now harvest the fruits of your toil. Just as the end of the day brought the promised jug of wine to the farmer in the field, so there are rewards – perhaps financial, perhaps less material – for your efforts in the past.

Dog This is a suitable moment for you to attend to your living environment. There are matters which need to be seen to, and which require urgent attention, or you may find yourself having to find new accommodation at short notice.

Pig This is not a favourable time to start new projects, whether in personal or business relationships. Such changes may not offer all they promised, leaving you in a difficult position.

OTHER ANIMAL INFLUENCES

How the other animal signs in the horoscope chart influence the Monkey

Rat A favourable sign to have in the horoscope, as it adds creative ingenuity to the mental processes. A successful career may involve head and hands.

Ox The Ox adds stability to an erratic way of life. There will be many changes of location but this Monkey will always yearn to return home.

Tiger (Post Horse) The Post Horse is in a difficult position. There are strong reasons for leaving home to live and work in a foreign land. Ties with family may be completely severed.

Rabbit This sign adds romance and compassion, and a love of those who cannot care for themselves. It suggests a career teaching or as a veterinarian.

Dragon A very auspicious sign. This person has charisma and flair, and will frequently be in the public eye. An extravagant lifestyle needs control.

Snake Thoughtful mental processes enhance the Monkey's skills. Such a person is good at analysing people and situations, eliciting information which can be commercially useful.

Horse A friendly, sociable character, either out with friends or inviting them home. Generally popular, but unfortunately certain aspects of character do not charm everybody.

Sheep Family life is important, and much of this Monkey's efforts are directed to ensuring that all are comfortable.

Monkey Despite strong self-confidence, some aspects of life are neglected. Being driven to achieve a goal can often blind you to more pressing issues.

Rooster (Flower of Love) Though capable of maintaining a loving partnership, one relationship is never quite enough. Discretion is thrown to the wind.

Dog Efforts are channelled into the creation of a highly individual home. The decor may be unsurprising, but the house may have curiously constructed rooms and walls.

Pig Handicraft skills can be developed. Applying your gifts to the manufacture and distribution of household items would be profitable.

THE ROOSTER

HOUSE: *Career*
BRANCH: X / *Yin*
ELEMENT: *Metal*

The animal chosen to represent the tenth sign was the chicken (usually called the Rooster), because the tenth hour (5 pm – 7 pm) was the time when the chickens came home to roost. Once the evening meal had been eaten and some wine drunk, the evening would usually be spent relaxing with some kind of entertainment. Today it tends to be television; then, it may have been playing or listening to music, reading or painting. Such activities require a certain amount of skill, which is why the Rooster represents artistic abilities more related to the enjoyment and enhancement of leisure hours, rather than to the useful machinery and functional gadgetry which properly belong to the Monkey's sphere.

PERSONALITY

The personal qualities associated with the Rooster are skills in music, art, literature, and all matters which pertain to enjoyment rather than necessity. A markedly feminine sign, it is nevertheless a very strong one, and shows force of character and determination. It also shows a strong emotional nature, fond of social activity, and one which is not afraid of putting a point of view forward. It is a sign of good business sense, showing that the way to financial security and wealth begins by first developing connoisseurship and knowledge of the fine arts.

COMPATIBILITY

How people born in the year of the Rooster relate to people born in the different animal years

Rat These two have a lot to offer each other, but they both have different goals, and their priorities may not always match. They can be very happy together, but it is advisable to have an escape route at the ready. The Rooster may feel that the Rat is not giving enough, while the Rat may think the Rooster too demanding.

Ox This could be an agreeable relationship – the Ox is one of the Rooster's two ideal partners. However, Ox personalities tend to be set in their ways, while the Rooster prefers change. But, once the Ox has decided the Rooster can offer constructive companionship, their affinity is sealed.

Tiger Two strong-minded individuals, who have their own priorities, and are unwilling to change them. In committing to each other, it is best to question each other's motives for embarking on a partnership. It is important to be honest with each other.

Rabbit The bonds which tie this couple are loose. They are likely to have come from different backgrounds, and often there can be a lack of communication between them. Though their different viewpoints and ambitions may cause anguish, they never seem to air their differences. Perhaps some cooperation and compromise would help to strengthen their affinity.

Dragon Both are such unpredictable characters that some foundation of stability is very important if they are to survive as individuals, let alone as a couple. It is important to guard against making decisions which could cause financial insecurity.

Snake This may be the true partner for the Rooster. Both have an eye for the finer things in life and, while they share many interests, they also have sufficiently different tastes and attitudes to keep their mutual admiration burning. Their many friends may regard them as an inseparable couple, though their careers may be independent.

Horse These are two lively characters who independently have many friends. But the admiration they get is perhaps due to the fact that their personalities are only ladled out in small portions. The mutual attraction that brought these two together can fade when given too much exposure.

Sheep This couple may have known each other for some time before their affection drew them together. The roles of home-maker and breadwinner may be reversed in this relationship, which could be regarded by others as somewhat unconventional. Happiness, nevertheless, is assured.

Monkey Being opposite poles of the same magnet, this couple are so close that they are not satisfied just with being partners at home – they may work together as well. Their objectives are shared, and any differences between them are soon resolved. Indeed, there is an eagerness to understand and participate in the other partner's activities.

Rooster This is one of the few signs which is weakened, rather than strengthened, by repetition. Two Roosters would be too close in spirit to be able to harmonize. They see their own foibles and shortcomings only too clearly in their partner, which makes it difficult to justify finding fault in each other.

Dog On the surface, there seems to be a good match of partners here, since they have so many similar interests. But, deep down, there are different long-term objectives in their lives. One is happy to stay at home and improve the existing situation, but the other partner's sights are set on the horizon. Think about the future.

Pig A contented life together, and a prosperous business, lead to a stable relationship which offers all the pleasures of a comfortable and well-ordered home. Family life is relaxed but organized, and the couple can look forward to many years of satisfied tranquillity that many would envy.

FAVOURABLE AND UNFAVOURABLE PERIODS

How the Rooster fares in periods ruled by the different animal signs

Rat A sticky period, with difficulties where numbers are concerned. These are not problems which cause long-term anxiety. Not a good time to begin new projects, unless short-term.

Ox A favourable period, which may involve moving. If this is in a south-easterly direction, so much the better. Any new ideas, or personal commitments, can be undertaken with confidence.

Tiger Not a good time to get into arguments with people in authority, as the outcome may not be worth the effort. Do not try to prove a point, as this will only infuriate your opponent and make your position more uncomfortable.

Rabbit This period is best used as a time for reviewing your present position, and seeing what will be the best course of action in the future. It is not a favourable time to start any new business, embark on a new relationship or move house.

Dragon Matters appear to be moving smoothly, but you may be tempted to take an unsound course of action. Use common sense rather than misguided inspiration.

Snake A very profitable period if you coordinate your resources and make your move. Any legal papers should be signed and formalized during this positive phase. If you are thinking of beginning a new partnership, you can go ahead with confidence.

Horse You may find colleagues difficult to work with. Some people are very set in their ways and ideas. Try to be patient. Neither dismiss their ideas nor accept them. Any problems will resolve themselves eventually.

Sheep Quite a productive phase. Matters should proceed without outside interference – let them take their course. You will be able to delegate responsibilities and have some time to relax.

Monkey Anything to do with personal improvement, whether physical or mental, will bring positive results. A time when you can develop your own skills and achieve a secret ambition.

Rooster Although you are ruled by your own sign, the Chinese refer to this as the 'Attack of the Self'. There may be problems which prevent you reaching your goal. Personal health is important, so don't expose yourself to the risk of injury or illness.

Dog A period in which to consider positive improvements to your environment. House extensions are a possibility, or you might add to your living space in other ways. A change of location, however, is not advised.

Pig This is a favourable period for family matters: gatherings and reunions bring not just personal satisfaction but, through surprise meetings, the prospect of career or financial advancement as well.

OTHER ANIMAL INFLUENCES

How the other animal signs in the horoscope chart influence the Rooster

Rat The artistic flair which is already in evidence is given a creative boost by the inclusion of the Rat sign. It provides an improved ability to concentrate and work out your plans in precise detail.

Ox A steadying influence which brings practical sense to a somewhat exotic lifestyle. The ability to persevere and get results is one that is much to be admired by others.

Tiger An abrasive style may not win friends, but will get you where you want to be in life. However, it is important to tread on the rungs of the ladder, and not on people's heads, as you make your way to the top.

Rabbit The diverse qualities of these two characters could be harnessed to good advantage, rather than being allowed to cause inner anxiety. Compartmentalize your life, so that you can proceed in your two directions without adverse effects.

Dragon Beware of being a spendthrift. Your intuition is remarkable but not always accurate. Make sure that your errors are not so substantial that they can be ruinous.

Snake An analytical mind gives great intellectual strength. Such a person might go into the law or politics. It is unlikely that your talents will be wasted.

Horse (Flower of Love) Personal relationships become too involved and complex. There is a conflict of interests between keeping a steady relationship and pursuing a new experience. Proceed carefully.

Sheep A useful ingredient in your personality is a touch of realistic foresight, which enables you to tread carefully between what is ideal and what is practicable.

Monkey An active and fertile imagination is coupled with the ability to put ideas into practice.

But avoid being too narrow-minded, and try to broaden your horizons.

Rooster The extra Rooster in the horoscope is a warning sign to avoid dependence on alcohol, medication or, worse, drugs (the ancient symbol for the tenth Chinese sign was a wine bottle). Also, avoid getting involved with people who are likely to fall prey to these dangers.

Dog You feel that life has much more to offer, and may occasionally feel depressed and frustrated by your lack of direction. But only you can do something about it; no one else will.

Pig (Post Horse) The Post Horse is placed in a favourable position, which indicates travel over long distances – in the third millennium, perhaps it signifies intercontinental commuting.

THE DOG

At the close of the day, before retiring for the night prudent householders check that doors are locked and windows secured. In past times, a watchman would be posted at the gate. Thus, the ancient icon for the eleventh sign – and hour – showed a hand holding a spear. The modern Chinese sign is more stylized and hardly recognizable, but the zodiac animal which has replaced it in popular literature is the Dog. Thus, the Dog reminds us that this sign represents protection and defence. Astrologically, it belongs to the House of Home Life, and specifically to the exterior of the home – which protects the family from wind and rain. By extension, it also refers to maintenance and repairs to the house itself.

PERSONALITY

It is easy to look at the image of the friendly house-dog and say that its attributes are loyalty and service, but the original meaning of this sign – a hand holding a spear – is a reminder that this dog is more of a German Shepherd guard dog than a French Poodle or Chihuahua! Fidelity does not mean weakness, or lack of mettle; rather, it demonstrates concern for those for whom there is a direct responsibility. As an extreme, this defensiveness might be expressed as jealousy. The obvious positive qualities of the Dog person are friendliness to those who are known and trusted, hospitality to guests, courage in adversity, and a dedicated application in their chosen career.

HOUSE: *Home Life*
BRANCH: XI / *Yang*
ELEMENT: *Earth*

COMPATIBILITY

How people born in the year of the Dog relate to people born in other animal years

Rat There is bound to be friction between two characters with distinctly different ways of doing things. While the Dog prefers to stay with the tried and trusted, the Rat wants to try new untested methods. But they are unlikely to let such problems stand in the way of their companionship.

Ox Only time will tell whether these two are meant for each other. They both find their partner can be traditionalist, instead of taking up life-improving opportunities. Outsiders may find their disagreements petty, and wonder why they allow apparently trifling matters to upset them so.

Tiger The Dog and Tiger have much in common. They may come from different backgrounds, but find that they both have similar views. Together they can work in harmony and achieve their objectives successfully. They can look forward to a long and prosperous life.

Rabbit Some couples would find this an uncomfortable relationship, as if something was missing from their lives. But perhaps when they have shared responsibilities they will have more to share than the physical attraction which first drew them together. Holding this partnership together may be hard work.

Dragon In order to preserve trust, it is important not to give grounds for suspicion. Whether in social relationships or financial dealings, it is important that there is no secrecy between these two. As much as the Dog would like to trust the Dragon, sometimes doubts may be justified, even if misplaced.

Snake These two are likely to proceed along their chosen routes, occasionally acknowledging the other's presence, taking comfort in the fact that their partner is there when the situation calls for it. They may not be open in displaying their fondness for each other, but this does not mean that deep feelings are not there.

Horse This partnership has an abundance of energy, with two ideally suited partners enjoying life together to the full. They have an enviable reputation as a fun-loving couple whose home and social life is to be coveted. They are popular among their friends, and bring laughter wherever they go.

Sheep This couple must learn to weather the storms of life. There are times when it is not possible to have everything, but there is a world of difference between what is needed and what is wanted. High expectations may lead to disappointment. They should take care of each other when times are lean.

Monkey A lively duo who take great comfort from each other's company. They are each able to get on with their own lives, but are pleased when the other takes the trouble to admire their efforts. Separation, perhaps through business commitments, is not a problem for them, though there is always delight when they are together again.

Rooster An old Chinese proverb declares this relationship a difficult one. They don't share the same priorities, and it is hard to sustain a partnership and build a future together when both partners have different expectations. Even in such trivial matters as interior decoration, they may disagree. Still, it can be worth making the effort.

Dog A happy home life and strong family ties ensure a long, stable relationship. These two take life one step at a time, making their way with increasing comfort and prosperity. There is such a close affinity between them that they seem to be able to read each other's minds.

Pig Being the opposite sides of the same coin, both belonging to the House of Home Life, this should be an ideal relationship for those wanting to establish a stable partnership. But there are hidden personality differences which can cause clashes. The more open they are with each other, the better life will be for both of them.

FAVOURABLE AND UNFAVOURABLE PERIODS

How the Dog fares in periods ruled by the different animal signs

Rat A period of growth and development, leading to a noticeably improved financial position. The time can be spent usefully in redistributing assets, and reorganizing time to benefit from new opportunities.

Ox Obstacles stand in the way of progress. These are not permanent hindrances, but can seriously delay plans all the same. In many ways, it might be better to hold your ground for the moment, rather than to change direction. Use the time for consolidating resources.

Tiger A fruitful period when it is advisable to move swiftly. Prospects are highly promising, and whether the question of the moment is about a career move, a new relationship or a change of location, the time is ripe. South-west is a favourable direction at this time.

Rabbit It would be unwise to make any major plans for this period, as there could be problems regarding a colleague's health. Unexpected family commitments may possibly stand in the way, occasioning last-minute cancellations.

Dragon This is not a favourable time to take risks, especially where financial investment is involved. Gambling may lead to a great loss. Plans which involve reliance on another party should be treated with caution, as the prospects do not match the promises made.

Snake There is opposition to your plans, which you may not be aware of. It would be wise to delay any action until you are fully aware of the potential hazards it may bring about. At the moment you are not in full possession of the facts.

Horse You can proceed with confidence at this time. This a highly favourable and productive period, in which you can realize a long-standing ambition. You may embark on a fresh career or find a new romance in your life. You will be in much demand at social functions.

Sheep Rather than trying to look beyond your present horizons, concentrate on issues which are not so ambitious. The solution you are seeking may be much closer than you had realized. Don't dismiss the advice of someone just because you are too familiar with them.

Monkey While there is a very optimistic atmosphere during this stimulating period in your life, don't allow yourself to be carried away on a wave of enthusiasm. The benefits that are promised may not be as helpful as you had hoped.

Rooster In business, and in your personal life too, you may find that there is a rival who stands in the way of your success. It may cause anguish at first, but you will soon come to realize that your aspirations were misplaced.

Dog Since this sign matches your own, it is a phase when you can start afresh. You can embark with confidence on a fresh venture, even if it involves a complete re-think of your life. South is a favourable direction for relocation.

Pig A refreshingly quiet period when you can set family matters to rights. A house move will proceed more smoothly than you expected. A long-standing grievance in the family will be healed, and new bonds forged.

OTHER ANIMAL INFLUENCES

How the other animal signs in the horoscope chart influence the Dog

Rat A creative mind may be kept in check by a desire to be seen as conventional. A yearning to travel may be unfulfilled because of commitments.

Ox Living in leased or rented accommodation is dissatisfying. Dealings with property and a constant need to expand is a driving force throughout life.

Tiger The voice of authority speaks. Such a person is likely to have a flair for organization, and may even play a part in government service.

Rabbit (Flower of Love) Casual relationships not only cause anxiety, but can be dangerous. But the frisson of an illicit affair may be impossible to avoid. Tread with care: a Tiger lives next door.

Dragon Be sensible about expenditure. Don't try to get rich quick. You must resist the temptation to invest in fancy schemes.

Snake The surface personality is a hearty and cheerful everyday one, but beneath this surface there lies a clever manipulator who has accumulated many interesting secrets.

Horse Lively and companionable, this popular person is often called upon to organize social events. An involvement in committee work is highly probable.

Sheep This reveals someone who is likely to be a strong defender of the vulnerable. Being too defensive in acting for the supposed rights of others may sometimes bring problems.

Monkey (Post Horse) Travel for pleasure and the improvement of a comfortable lifestyle. Temporary residence in a foreign country may eventually be permanent.

Rooster Do not take offence at criticism when it is meant kindly. You have talents and gifts, and as these improve you may see that previous efforts were not as good as you had thought.

Dog By concentrating too much on the details, the bigger picture may be overlooked. Stand back and reassess your position.

Pig Home life and business are nicely integrated. Your ideal position would be a career which enables you to work from home, but try to draw a distinction between the two.

THE PIG

The twelfth zodiac sign represents the onset of night. Its original meaning has been lost, although the accepted view is that it represented a boar, which may explain why the Pig was chosen when animal names were adopted. Perhaps a boar was chosen for the last hour of the day, as its grunting sounded like a family snoring happily. Family security and contentment are also expressed in the Chinese character for 'family', which shows a pig under a roof. Add a man to the combination of pig and roof, and you have the Chinese character for 'carpentry'. Add a woman, and the character represents marriage. All these qualities – contentedness, home security, family life, furnishings – are contained in this sign.

PERSONALITY

Unsurprisingly, not everyone born in the year of the Pig is flattered by the thought. However, Pig types are among the nicest people you could hope to meet. They have all the qualities needed to bring happiness into their homes and, though they may be content to stay there, they have no hesitation in inviting friends and strangers to share their happiness. But this may also be one of their failings, for they are so concerned with the welfare of others that they tend to take people at face value. Unfortunately, they can become prey to the unscrupulous, and be easily tricked or swindled.

Ever eager to make their homes the height of comfort and good living, their cupboards will be full of all kinds of ornaments and gadgets that might be used once and put away. Because they are so keen to create a luxurious, stable home, they are reliable workers, not afraid to make the extra effort when their services are needed.

HOUSE: *Home Life*
BRANCH: XII / *Yin*
ELEMENT: *Water*

COMPATIBILITY

How people born in the year of the Pig relate to people born in the different animal years

Rat Although these two personalities are outwardly close, they have many differences which sometimes act as a barrier between them. The Rat may feel restless, wanting to be on the move, while the Pig partner is content with the present position. A little bit of give and take is needed in this relationship.

Ox There is a good rapport between these two. They are both keen to make their home the envy of their friends, with the Ox partner always wishing that they had more space for the family to grow. If this couple were also in business together, much of their work would be home-based.

Tiger Their objectives do not always lie in the same direction. Perhaps it would be best if business and home life were made quite distinct. While this may not be a positive step towards bringing them closer together, it does stop the creation of disputes and tensions between them, which are helpful to neither.

Rabbit When two people have such similar interests, and are able to share their lives with such companionship and joy, love and happiness is bound to grow. This is a warm and fulfilling partnership. Attention to money matters will ensure that they have home comforts and financial security to fall back on.

Dragon Do not be too easily swayed by the magnetic attraction of the Dragon, who has ambitions beyond the Pig's experience and may resent the Pig's observations of what is realistic. Patience and understanding can pay off eventually.

Snake The Pig does its best to provide a comfortable environment for the Snake, and the Snake does its best to repay its gratitude. But there is still something missing in their life together, as if their lives never overlap. Perhaps they should be happy as they are, and not try to make the situation better.

Horse This couple will lead a comfortable life, following their own paths and respecting each other's judgement. This is likely to be a relationship between two gifted and intelligent people, often of independent means, who see the advantages that this partnership brings them.

Sheep An extremely favourable relationship, which the Chinese astrologers of old declared to be one of the most felicitous of all. It is strongly home – and family based – and can also be a prosperous business relationship. Family life is rewarding, and children will bring honours in middle age.

Monkey Outside the home, these two can enjoy each other's company heartily. Both are fun-loving people, who like to enjoy an active social life. But in a domestic environment, trouble is likely to brew. Both have different views regarding domestic priorities, and what is important for one is often a triviality for the other. Differences are best unravelled outside the home.

Rooster This partnership has all the ingredients for a happy and prosperous life together. It is best to separate business and leisure, however. Although they may have different ambitions, both partners are keen to know what progress the other is making in their chosen career. The secret of their success is the informal way they organize their time apart and together.

Dog At home, or in business, these two are a happy complement for each other. But, being so close, they may miss the opportunities which lie beyond the horizon. This partnership, though favourable, always works better when there is a third party (perhaps a younger family member) to open their eyes to new possibilities.

Pig Such similar people should have no problems together. But there is the nub of the difficulty: they may be single-minded in reaching their objectives, but resentful of their partner treading the same route. It only needs one person to sweep a step.

FAVOURABLE AND UNFAVOURABLE PERIODS

How the Pig fares in periods ruled by the different animal signs

Rat A period of upheaval and change, whether this is wanted or not, so it would be advisable to be flexible when planning for the immediate future. Some rearrangement of your finances would be in order.

Ox A stable period when matters will proceed as expected. Plans involving land or expansion of home or business premises receive favourable attention. Problems outside the home can be resolved satisfactorily.

Tiger A difficult period which might bring you into conflict with superiors or government officials. If you intend to do anything likely to need official approval, draft applications punctiliously.

Rabbit An extremely favourable period, generating a stimulating and inspiring atmosphere. Use the time constructively, and do not waste a moment. Help will come to you from an unexpected source if you are bold enough to ask.

Dragon Make sure you have enough reserves to cope with emergencies. The chance to achieve a lifelong ambition will come your way, but whether you take the opportunity depends on how well you have prepared for the unexpected.

Snake Normally, a sign in such a powerfully opposed position suggests a difficult situation. But the Chinese say – 'The Pig eats the Snake', so these problems will be resolved if you attack them head-on.

Horse You may encounter problems in balancing the demands of home life and career. Male family members can cause disputes, but these can be resolved with the help of people who are known to them.

Sheep A very profitable year, allowing you to indulge yourself. Your social life will flourish. If you are hoping to embark on a new relationship, you will find this a most rewarding period.

Monkey Minor irritations may cause setbacks. People you had relied on might not provide the support you expect. If you buy mechanical equipment, make sure the guarantee lasts for more than a year.

Rooster While your home and domestic life remains comfortably stable, there are more opportunities for you to enjoy life outside the house. An entertaining visitor enters your life temporarily – perhaps someone from abroad who wishes to stay.

Dog This a period of support and encouragement. You may proceed with your plans, and are able to find time for self-development. For once, you feel justified in ignoring those who do not share your views.

Pig Take care not to concentrate on one aspect of your life. This is a period when it will be beneficial to throw unwanted baggage overboard and see what you can do without.

OTHER ANIMAL INFLUENCES

How the other animal signs in the horoscope chart influence the Pig

Rat (Flower of Love) Conversational fluency in this character means that this person is a good talker, but may not be such a good listener. The desire to put a view forward may manifest itself in letter-writing or journalism.

Ox Acquisitiveness can lead to a shortage of space. Life is driven by a need to find larger accommodation. At times, it may seem as though the quest will never end. A career as an estate agent might provide the opportunity to realize the fantasy of living in a castle.

Tiger Hard work and the pressures of home life are apt to try your patience. Fortunately, in situations like this you are able to exercise authority tempered with understanding.

Rabbit Your positive qualities are enhanced, but so are the less favourable ones of naivety and gullibility. It is good to care for others, but better when they care for you as well.

Dragon The prospects for investment are not favourable in this instance – an apparent flair for turning over a fortune may prove to be illusory, and the result of earlier lucky strikes. Speculate carefully.

Snake (Post Horse) It is hard to balance kindness with cynicism, but it is to your credit that you can see when others are really in need, and when they are merely trying to take advantage of your generous nature.

Horse Although you ideally like to work from your home base, you are not afraid to travel further afield – into previously unexplored territory – when the situation demands. This is to your advantage.

Sheep This caring personality will be much sought after for advice and comfort when others are facing difficulties. Despite the incursions into private time, the eventual rewards are very gratifying.

Monkey There are times when your practical skills are much in demand. Make sure that you know the value of your services, and that your time is properly appreciated, or you may come to resent being taken for granted.

Rooster There is an exotic quality about this person. Lurking beneath an outwardly traditional image, there is an unsuspected streak of daring which can spring surprises.

Dog A very integrated person, self-sufficient but also sometimes appearing rather distant. There may be a friendliness towards others, but a discreet distance is always maintained in social relationships.

Pig It is important to experience as much as possible of the world, and to meet with people from as many different backgrounds. Avoid being partisan and prejudgemental.

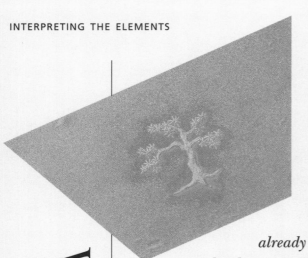

WOOD

木

TYPE: *Yang Wood*
QUALITY: *Trees*
STEM: 1 / *Jia*

TYPE: *Yin Wood*
QUALITY: *Grass*
STEM: 2 / *Yi*

The Wood element rules over all vegetation. This is the creative element of nature. Associated with spring, it suggests new life, birth and caring, and thus is the most feminine and gentle of the elements. Yang Wood represents strength and the upright. It is the planting of seed – the moment of conception. Yin Wood is a seed already planted and sprouting, and signifies development. The classics say that, during a Wood period, the emperor should bestow favours and refrain from cutting. In modern terms, it is a time to help others and to heal through the use of medicines.

PRODUCES	
FIRE	*Harmonious*
IS PRODUCED BY	
WATER	*Favourable*
DESTROYS	
EARTH	*Discordant*
IS DESTROYED BY	
METAL	*Unfavourable*

FIRE

WOOD — EARTH

WATER — METAL

PERSONALITY

Wood-type people reveal their creative ability in many ways. They support those less fortunate than themselves. As pioneers, they push forward – not for their own fame and glory, but in order to make a more perfect world. They make good leaders and managers, as they feel it is important to gain the cooperation of others, rather than imposing rules and regulations for the sake of discipline.

The Yang Wood type is the more creative of the two types, and is a great starter, but likes others to complete the task. On the other hand, the Yin Wood type is more adept at developing other people's ideas in a practical way. The emotion of Wood is anger, and such people may be prone to displays of temper when pent-up frustrations burst out. Physically, Wood types are of a tall, slim build with slender fingers and an upright bearing.

HOW TO REVITALIZE WOOD

To enhance your Wood element, emphasize green and light blue in your surroundings. Vertical stripes and accessories or ornaments which are narrow and tall stimulate the effect of the Wood element. Yang Wood is enhanced by plants which are growing and thriving, and by the east direction. Yin Wood is stimulated by dried plants and objects made of bamboo or paper, and by the south-east direction. An appropriate drink would be lime juice. For greater stimulation, introduce the Water element (*see pages 82–3*).

OBSERVATIONS BASED ON THE ELEMENT WEIGHTING

0	1	2–3	4+
Without the creative Wood element, this person needs instruction and order. With direction, they may be fastidious and particular; without it, completely disorganized. Often there is a lack of interest in vital matters, at its worst descending into a listless apathy. Enhance the Wood or Water elements as suggested below, left.	The presence of the Wood element shows a well-balanced creative side. This character has helpful qualities, shown by concern for family welfare and an eagerness to please. These people are always on the lookout for new ideas.	The creative quality is strongly marked, revealing an artistic streak that reacts positively to stimulating company. Other people's ideas can be reformed constructively. There are good leadership and management skills – a commendable trait.	A superabundance of the Wood element makes the creative side too dominant. The effect of this can be a fractious and unpredictable temper. This character is highly imaginative, but with too many ideas and fanciful ambitions. There is a danger of being a dreamer without the capability to put plans into action. You can reduce the Wood influence by introducing the Fire element into the surroundings.

MEANING OF OTHER ELEMENTS

Growing vegetation draws its nourishment from the soil. For someone whose Day Element is Wood, Earth is the element which supplies the wealth. The same sign element (Yang Earth for Yang Wood) indicates wealth that was acquired by accident, good luck, or otherwise unexpectedly. The reverse sign (Yang Earth for Yin Wood, and vice versa) reveals the wealth which is arrived at through hard work. Being in Earth, it suggests that land and estate are the sources of a comfortable lifestyle for the Wood person.

As Metal chops down Wood, this is an unfavourable sign in the horoscope when its polarity matches that of the Day Element (Yang Metal with Yang Wood). On the other hand, it can produce a beneficial change if the polarity is different (*see table below*).

IMPORTANT FACTORS TO LOOK FOR IN THE HOROSCOPE CHART

DAY ELEMENT	UNEXPECTED WEALTH	EARNED WEALTH	HAPPINESS	UNFAVOURABLE SIGN	BENEFICIAL CHANGE
Yang Wood	*Yang Earth*	*Yin Earth*	*Yin Water*	*Yang Metal*	*Yin Metal*
Yin Wood	*Yin Earth*	*Yang Earth*	*Yang Water*	*Yin Metal*	*Yang Metal*

FIRE

火

TYPE: *Yang Fire*

QUALITY: *Furnace*

STEM: *3 / Bing*

TYPE: *Yin Fire*

QUALITY: *Candle*

STEM: *4 / Ding*

*F*ire is the element of summer and the south. It is a time when growth is at its most prolific, a time of optimism and joyous anticipation. Yang Fire is the burning furnace for melting bronze, the kiln for firing pots, and the oven for baking bread. Yin Fire is the lambent candle flame that lightens the darkness, and the gentle warmth of the mother's breast. The Chinese classics warn against being too hurried during the Fire period: actions taken without due care may cause epidemics and drought. In health matters, Fire refers to the heart and circulation of the blood.

PRODUCES
EARTH
Harmonious

IS PRODUCED BY
WOOD
Favourable

DESTROYS
METAL
Discordant

IS DESTROYED BY
WATER
Unfavourable

PERSONALITY

Fire gives people intelligence, which often reveals itself in a quick wit and sparkling conversation. Fire types can be fervent and passionate, and surround themselves with like-minded people. They can inspire, expecting everyone else not only to share their enthusiasm, but to be as single-minded in their determination to succeed. Uncompromising in their demands, they may overlook the fact that other people have priorities of their own.

The Yang Fire person can be quite aggressive in their approach, and may use psychological bullying to achieve an objective. The Yin Fire type is likely to be more successful with others because of their ability to use humour. When faced with adversity, the Fire type's comic sense is a happy way to deflect conflict. The Fire physique is angular, with sharply defined features and a hurried gait.

HOW TO REVITALIZE FIRE

The Fire element is symbolized by the colour red and all related shades, such as russet and rose. Because red is such a vital colour, often just a splash of vermilion in an unexpected place is enough to stimulate the Fire element. The shape connected with the Fire element is triangular, and objects of a markedly pointed or angular shape also introduce the Fire quality. Hearths and stoves have a Yang Fire quality, while candles and soft lighting are Yin Fire, as is the scent of cloves. As an added curiosity, the drink Campari, with its bitter taste and red colour, amply symbolizes the Fire element. The appropriate direction or location for such enhancements is the south.

OBSERVATIONS BASED ON THE ELEMENT WEIGHTING

0	1	2–3	4+
If there is no Fire element in the basic horoscope chart, it reveals a tendency to remain with the family group. Sometimes when people are talking together, it is difficult to grasp the underlying meaning, as if the vital point had been missed. There is an inclination to be over-serious and pious. Ways to enhance the Fire element are suggested below, left.	A balanced proportion of Fire in the horoscope suggests level-headedness. Important matters are dealt with sensibly and practically. In business, this character would make a good intermediary or agent.	A strong personality, with infectious humour that draws an appreciative circle of friends. This person has a sense of fun that is vigorous without being offensive. They have a keen eye to spot opportunities which are ready to be developed, even though it means persuading others to provide the resources.	With so much Fire, such types can burn themselves out too easily. A rather raucous sense of humour may not meet with universal appreciation. Potential problems lie with the circulatory system. Reduce the effect by introducing the Earth element into the immediate environment when appropriate, but do not attempt to quench the Fire with Water.

MEANING OF OTHER ELEMENTS

If the Day Element is Fire, Metal represents the person's wealth. Fire melts Metal, but does not destroy it. In fact, Fire is used to transform the unshaped Metal into something of greater value. Thus, wealth is in the control of the Fire person. For a Yang Fire person, Yang Metal in the horoscope indicates sudden wealth, while for the Yin Fire person it reveals the extent of the rewards for an active and industrious life. The reverse holds true regarding Yin Metal.

As Fire is quenched by Water, the appearance of the Water element with the same polarity (Yang or Yin) is not favourable, but if the Water has the opposite polarity it can bring benefits through travel and the written word (*see table below*).

IMPORTANT FACTORS TO LOOK FOR IN THE HOROSCOPE CHART

DAY ELEMENT	UNEXPECTED WEALTH	EARNED WEALTH	HAPPINESS	UNFAVOURABLE SIGN	BENEFICIAL CHANGE
Yang Fire	*Yang Metal*	*Yin Metal*	*Yin Wood*	*Yang Water*	*Yin Water*
Yin Fire	*Yin Metal*	*Yang Metal*	*Yang Wood*	*Yin Water*	*Yang Water*

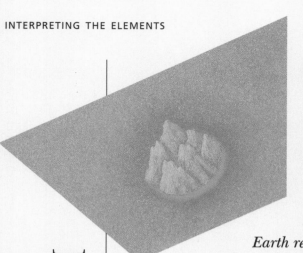

EARTH

土

TYPE: *Yang Earth*
QUALITY: *City Walls*
STEM: 5 / *Wu*

TYPE: *Yin Earth*
QUALITY: *Ditches*
STEM: 6 / *Ji*

The Earth element is concerned with the ground beneath our feet, and the uses to which it is put. Both firm and pliable, it is the land over which we roam and the soil in which our food grows. The colour of Earth is yellow, like the loess soil of central China. Yang Earth is symbolized by the rocks which build the city walls. Yin Earth represents the Earth which supports our growing food. The Earth period governs the last days of each season, particularly harvest time. In health terms Earth represents the workings of the digestive system, good health being assured by the right diet.

PRODUCES
METAL
Harmonious

IS PRODUCED BY
FIRE
Favourable

DESTROYS
WATER
Discordant

IS DESTROYED BY
WOOD
Unfavourable

FIRE

WOOD — EARTH

WATER — METAL

PERSONALITY

The enduring and immutable nature of Earth is revealed in people who are traditional in their ways, firm and reliable, and unlikely to be swayed by novelty. They are hard workers, their persistence and tenacity carrying them through the most arduous of tasks. Of course, they can be resolute and obstinate, and it is difficult to shake their determination to pursue their chosen objective.

The Yang Earth person may be more concerned with land as a medium for building, and the Yin Earth person, with its agricultural potential. The emotion ruled by Earth is rumination, revealed in Earth types by bouts of silent contemplation and meditative introspection. To strangers, they may seem distant, but it is not in their nature to make small talk. The physical Earth type is broad-shouldered and well-built, with strong hands.

HOW TO REVITALIZE EARTH

Yellows, ochres, stones, tiles and bricks all belong to the Earth element, as do flat surfaces and square or rectangular shapes. Orange juice, in both taste and colour, represents the Earth element. Chinese people are fond of naturally formed stones of fantastic shapes. The larger stones will be installed at a suitable spot in their garden, the treasured smaller ones placed as a focus for meditation on a writing desk. Modern Chinese follow the Western practice of collecting natural semi-precious stones, amethysts, rock crystals and the like, but the older traditions encouraged a preference for a smooth stone of grotesque shape to stimulate the imagination.

OBSERVATIONS BASED ON THE ELEMENT WEIGHTING

0	1	2–4	5+
When Earth is deficient in the horoscope, it suggests a lack of commitment. Without its practical quality, a person becomes restless and hyperactive, tending to tire of the existing situation before its potential has been fully realized. To rectify the imbalance, introduce the Earth or Fire elements into the environment as suggested below, left, and on page 76.	The Earth element is present and helps to stabilize the personality, but because Earth is central to the Four Directions it needs to be firm and strong. If there is only one Earth present, it is better when also supported by Fire.	Persistence and reliability are noticeable traits in this character. A good steady worker who earns the respect and admiration, not only of family and friends, but also of people in influential positions. But it is important not to be imposed upon.	When over half the chart is taken up with the Earth element, the other forces have little chance to reveal their influence. One possible hazard is a tendency towards depression, and a lack of enthusiasm to leave a small circle of friends and family. The Water element will help to reduce its heaviness, as will (to a lesser extent) the Metal element.

MEANING OF OTHER ELEMENTS

Fire is said to be the mother of Earth, not so much because fire leaves ash behind, but because ferocious volcanoes of fire are seen to throw vast mountains of lava and rocks. Fire, the mother, brings happiness to the person whose Day Element is Earth, if one element is Yang and the other Yin. Earth could not support the plants to grow, nor could the clay be moulded without Water. In this way, Water is the element representing Earth's success and wealth.

Wood will render Earth barren, so if there is Wood in the horoscope of someone whose Day Element is Earth, it will be unfavourable if the two elements are both Yang or both Yin. If one is Yang and the other Yin, it shows fairness of judgement (see table below).

IMPORTANT FACTORS TO LOOK FOR IN THE HOROSCOPE CHART

DAY ELEMENT	UNEXPECTED WEALTH	EARNED WEALTH	HAPPINESS	UNFAVOURABLE SIGN	BENEFICIAL CHANGE
Yang Earth	*Yang Water*	*Yin Water*	*Yin Fire*	*Yang Wood*	*Yin Wood*
Yin Earth	*Yin Water*	*Yang Water*	*Yang Fire*	*Yin Wood*	*Yang Wood*

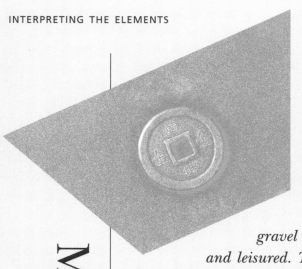

METAL 金

TYPE: *Yang Metal*
QUALITY: *Knives*
STEM: 7 / *Geng*

TYPE: *Yin Metal*
QUALITY: *Clasps*
STEM: 8 / *Xin*

The Metal element belongs to the autumn, signifying the setting sun, the west and matters concerning relaxation and entertainment. It also refers to the use of metal in weapons and the toil of reaping the harvest. The earth yields both hard ore (Yang Metal) used for iron and bronze utensils, and the soft gold from sandy river gravel (Yin Metal) for the adornment of the rich and leisured. The ancient belief was that the earth should not be attacked – ditches dug or foundations laid – during a Metal period. In health terms, Metal is favourable regarding surgical processes.

PRODUCES	**WATER** *Harmonious*
IS PRODUCED BY	**EARTH** *Favourable*
DESTROYS	**WOOD** *Discordant*
IS DESTROYED BY	**FIRE** *Unfavourable*

FIRE

WOOD — EARTH

WATER — METAL

PERSONALITY

There are two distinctive Metal types – the aggressive computer and the commercially astute. The Yang Metal person is driven by a need to succeed, and to outstrip rivals at whatever cost. The Yin Metal type is more interested in the fruits of success, and having time to enjoy them. Both types are keen to push themselves to the top, but the former is driven by principle, the latter by reward. Both are probably more interested in working for themselves to achieve their goals.

The emotion of Metal is grief. Despite a courageous veneer, Metal people have an inner sensitivity. Personal tragedy or lack of success affects them deeply, and they may give way to displays of their emotion. The Metal physique is muscular, with rounded features and high, but not angular, cheekbones, and a preference for keeping the hair short.

HOW TO REVITALIZE METAL

Autumn and the evening both pertain to the Metal element. It is symbolized by white and silver tones. The symbolic shape for Metal is round, like a coin, and all round shapes, such as bow windows, arches and circular frames, suggest the Metal element. Yang Metal is symbolized by knives and sharp implements; Yin Metal, by jewellery and trinkets. The appropriate direction for Yang Metal is the west, and for Yin Metal it is the north-west.

Metal is related to breathing and the nose. Thus, perfumes and incense belong to the Metal element. A mechanical clock also falls under the aegis of Metal, for its ability to stimulate this wealth-bringing element.

OBSERVATIONS BASED ON THE ELEMENTAL WEIGHTING

0	1	2–3	4+
The Metal element is needed to give ambition and self-esteem. Without it, this person needs to have constant reassurance and encouragement in order to succeed. It is important to balance kindness and sympathy with respect for oneself. Sometimes it is important to put yourself first for a change. The Earth element is needed to counteract the lack of Metal.	Metal is present in the horoscope in sufficient quantity to ensure that the personality is balanced as regards self-respect and ambition. In business dealings, the person is shrewd but fair. There is an attraction to sports and social pastimes, without being fanatical.	Aspects of the Metal element are distinct in character, but favourably so. Here is someone with ambition and drive, determined to succeed, and yet not too self-centred to forget friends. There is a strong competitive business streak – such people drive a hard bargain. Enterprise and eagerness are qualities that will ensure wealth in later years.	With so much Metal in the chart, edging out all the other essential factors, this person could be too single-minded. Aggressively competitive, such a self-possessed person is likely to use any means to justify the end. Acquaintances are apt to find them unsympathetic. At its worst, the strong Metal influence leads to maudlin self-pity. Reduce the Metal by introducing the Water element.

MEANING OF OTHER ELEMENTS

For someone whose Day Element is Metal, Earth is a particularly favourable element to see in the horoscope. There are a number of reasons for this. Earth, the mother of Metal, is supportive: Earth produces Metal. Metal is used to chop down trees, but in doing so it reshapes the Wood into something of greater utility. In this way, Wood serves Metal, and is the source of wealth in the horoscope.

The attacker of Metal is Fire. A Fire element with the same polarity (yin or yang) as the Day Element is dangerous, suggesting conflagration. But Yin Fire, which can be used to warm, or can be as soft as candlelight, is regarded as favourable when the Day Element is Yang Metal, and only slightly less so when the Metal element itself is also yin.

IMPORTANT FACTORS TO LOOK FOR IN THE HOROSCOPE CHART

DAY ELEMENT	UNEXPECTED WEALTH	EARNED WEALTH	HAPPINESS	UNFAVOURABLE SIGN	BENEFICIAL CHANGE
Yang Metal	Yang Wood	Yin Wood	Yin Earth	Yang Fire	Yin Fire
Yin Metal	Yin Wood	Yang Wood	Yang Earth	Yin Fire	Yang Fire

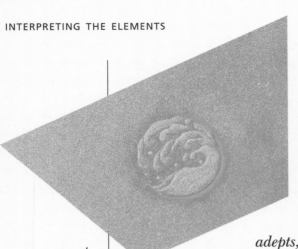

WATER

水

TYPE: *Yang Water*
QUALITY: *Rivers*
STEM: *9 / Ren*

TYPE: *Yin Water*
QUALITY: *Pools*
STEM: *10 / Gui*

The Water element encompasses water in all its manifestations. Liquids such as oil and alcohol – not materially water – were considered by the ancients to belong to this element. Metal produces Water through the action of Fire, which causes it to flow like water. What, in nature, is Yang and what is Yin is disputed by Chinese feng shui adepts, but does not affect the interpretation of a horoscope. The classics define the first quality of water as 'cleansing', and it has always been a medium for transport. Water, therefore, symbolizes the medium for all communication systems.

PRODUCES	**WOOD** *Harmonious*
IS PRODUCED BY	**METAL** *Favourable*
DESTROYS	**FIRE** *Discordant*
IS DESTROYED BY	**EARTH** *Unfavourable*

FIRE

WOOD   EARTH

WATER   METAL

PERSONALITY

Communication, writing, learning and travel are all important in different ways to the Water person. Water people make good intermediaries, and are likely to be drawn to careers in public relations.

Of the two Water types, the Yang Water person is likely to be more self-motivated, with the urge to communicate expressed in travelling. Outwardly fluent and a good talker, there is likely to be an inner coldness. In ancient times, the Yin Water day was set aside for communicating with spirits. Yin Water people may have psychic powers and deep feelings, which may not be apparent to outsiders.

Water people may like travelling, but won't take unnecessary risks. They prefer charted courses rather than dangerous enterprises. Physically, the Water person has a flexible way of moving, is a good dancer and has interesting asymmetrical features.

HOW TO REVITALIZE WATER

It is not necessary to have fountains, goldfish bowls and fishponds in order to stimulate the Water element. The 'Classic of Gardens' says that stones and rocks can be placed to give the impression of Water. In the inner environment, Water can be suggested by the relevant colour, which is normally dark blue or black. This need not be funereal, since it is only necessary to have the occasional splash of navy blue on a lighter background for the colour to startle and stimulate. Irregular shapes and wavy patterns belong to the Water element, and these could be a feature of fabrics and accessories. The sound of tinkling bells is also associated with the Water element.

OBSERVATIONS BASED ON THE ELEMENTAL WEIGHTING

0	1	2–3	4+
Without Water as the element of communication, there may be difficulty in expressing thoughts. Such people tend to have little sense of danger, and their recklessness is often mistaken for bravery. Taking little care for personal safety, they are accident prone. It is beneficial if there is Metal in the horoscope to remedy the imbalance; otherwise, stimulate the Water element, as suggested below, left.	An element of Water in the horoscope reveals someone who is a good questioner, rather than someone prone to giving replies at great length. This person is a good communicator, keeping conversation terse, but lucid.	This is a good balance of Water in the horoscope – enough for the qualities of communication skills to be noticeably entertaining. Anecdotes can be recounted with eloquence. There is a yearning to travel, and career choice is likely to have been influenced by the possibility to expand horizons.	An overload of Water in the chart suggests a desire to be free from commitments. There are unresolved personal issues and doubts, which can lead to anxieties and irrational fears. Conversation at times may appear inconsequential, and at other times bombastic. The Water element needs to be reduced by introducing Wood into the environment, or contained with Earth.

MEANING OF OTHER ELEMENTS

Water is used to control Fire, so it is the more dominant element of the two. When the Day Element of the horoscope is Water, Fire is the element that indicates wealth. If both elements are identically yang or yin, the wealth will be the result of a legacy or some other singular source. If the two elements have the opposite polarities, it shows the rewards for an industrious life.

Metal, which is said to produce Water, indicates satisfaction and happiness with one's life. Earth, which restrains or pollutes Water, may signify danger from accident or collisions if the two elements have the same polarity, but signifies a beneficial change in lifestyle if they are of opposite polarity (*see table below*).

IMPORTANT FACTORS TO LOOK FOR IN THE HOROSCOPE CHART

DAY ELEMENT	UNEXPECTED WEALTH	EARNED WEALTH	HAPPINESS	UNFAVOURABLE SIGN	BENEFICIAL CHANGE
Yang Water	*Yang Fire*	*Yin Fire*	*Yin Metal*	*Yang Earth*	*Yin Earth*
Yin Water	*Yin Fire*	*Yang Fire*	*Yang Metal*	*Yin Earth*	*Yang Earth*

THE LIFE CYCLE DECADES

The Life Cycle Decades are perhaps the most fascinating aspect of Chinese astrology. They reveal that there is more to the Chinese horoscope chart than just discovering what influences shape a person's character and personality. In fact, the chart is just the starting point from which the whole of your life and destiny can be unravelled. Once you have set up the chart, you can begin to compare the factors of the horoscope itself – the animal signs and the elements present – with those that come to bear at different periods of a lifetime.

Chinese astrology divides each person's life into separate periods of ten years known as 'Life Cycle Decades'. Each of these decades is said to be equivalent to a 'month' of a person's life. Since each of these Life Months has its own animal sign and element, these can be compared with a person's basic horoscope chart to determine whether a particular ten-year period is going to be a successful one, or an uphill struggle. Not only that, the Life Cycle Decades may even reveal the actual age in one's life when the various influences are favourable or otherwise.

Armed with this route-map, we are able to see what directions are the most favourable in our journey through life: when to expect problems and upheavals, and when would be the most effective moment to press ahead with important decisions, such as plans to move house, change career, or even to marry.

NOTE: *In traditional Chinese horoscopes, the Life Cycle Decades are written in adjacent columns. For our use, it is much easier – and more convenient – to write the decades one below the other.*

How to Calculate Life Cycle Decades

*F*irst, photocopy or copy the front flap of the chart booklet. Take a pen, and follow the step-by-step instructions below – you will need to have the person's horoscope chart handy.

1 Initial preparations Using the list of details set out, fill in the following:
(a) The person's name, date of birth and sex.
(b) From the horoscope chart, note whether the birth year is yang or yin.
(c) The stem element, animal sign and element of the animal sign for the month of birth (cards 3 and 4).
(d) The stem element for the day of birth (card 6).

2 Forward or backward movement The Life Cycle Decades move either forwards or backwards *(see also Step 4)*. For now, the first thing to determine is the direction of the movement – forwards or backwards. To do this, first note whether the birth year is yang or yin; then note whether the person's sex is yang (male) or yin (female). If the polarity (whether yang or yin) of the birth year and the person's sex are the same, the movement is forward. If they are different, the movement is backward. Write this down in the list.
• *Remember: same polarity = forward movement / different polarity = backward movement*

3 Determining the Natal Decade The Natal Decade is the decade in which a person was born. The stem and branch for the Natal Decade, expressed as the stem element and the animal sign, are the same as those for the month in which the person was born.

Write the data for the Natal Decade in your table in the appropriate boxes alongside 'Natal'.
• *Remember: Natal Decade data same as that for birth month*

4 Reckoning the numbers for the Life Cycle Decades Now turn to the Cycle of Sixty chart on page 5 in the chart booklet. Each combination of stem element and animal sign has a Cyclical Number – a figure from 1 to 60. Find the Cyclical Number which matches the Natal Decade (or birth month) data. Write this number in the No. column, alongside 'Natal'.

The numbers for the successive Life Cycle Decades follow on from this number, either increasing or decreasing according to whether the movement is forward or backward. If the movement (see Step 2) is *forward*, complete the No. column with ascending numbers, but if the movement is *backward*, complete the No. column with descending numbers. (Remember that the numbers are cyclical, so when you reach 60 you continue with 1, 2, 3 etc., and vice versa.)

EXAMPLE: *If the Cyclical Number for the Natal Decade (and birth month) is 57, and the movement is forward, you would continue the column with the numbers 58, 59, 60, 1, 2, 3, 4, 5. If, however, the Cyclical Number is 4 and the movement is backward, you would continue the column with the numbers 3, 2, 1, 60, 59, 58, 57, 56.*
• *Remember: forward movement numbers = ascending / backward movement numbers = descending*

5 Adding the elements and animal signs Having filled in the No. column, now fill in the stem element, animal sign and its own element for each decade, using the Cycle of Sixty chart on page 5 in the chart booklet.

6 Calculating the age at which each decade begins Now you need to find the actual age at which each of the Life Cycle Decades begins. Each solar month represents one decade of a person's life. But, while a decade is ten years, a solar month is (approximately) thirty days. So, if thirty days of a solar month represents ten years of a person's life, three days of a solar month are equivalent to one year of a person's life. See right for a reminder of the dates on which the Chinese solar months begin.

The next step depends on whether the movement is forward or backward.

(a) Forward Movement
If the movement is forward, count the number of days which elapse between the person's birthday and the start of the next solar month.
EXAMPLE: *If the person's birthday is 20 January, and the movement is forward, you count from 20 January to 4 February (the beginning of the next solar month). Thus: 21, 22, 23 Jan etc., to 1, 2, 3, 4 Feb = 15 days.*

(b) Backward Movement
If the movement is backward, count the number of days between the person's birthday and the beginning of the solar month in which the birthday occurred.
EXAMPLE: *If the person's birthday is 2 March, and the movement is backward, you count from 2 March back to 4 February (the beginning of the solar month containing the birthday). Thus: 1 Mar, 28, 27, 26 Feb etc., to 4 Feb = 26 days.*

NOTE: When counting, the birthday is ignored, because we are reckoning the amount of time which has elapsed

SOLAR MONTH DATES
• *6 January*
• *4 February*
• *5 March*
• *4 April*
• *5 May*
• *5 June*
• *7 July*
• *7 August*
• *7 September*
• *8 October*
• *7 November*
• *7 December*

between the two dates. The first day of the solar month, however, is counted. Also, make sure you note whether or not the birth year is a leap year, as this will affect the number of days that are counted for February.

(c) Calculating the First Decade

Now divide the number of elapsed days calculated in Step 6a or 6b by 3, rounding to the nearest whole number. This figure represents the age at which the first decade begins.

EXAMPLE (a): *15 days elapsed between the birthday and the start of the next solar month. 15 divided by 3 = 5, so the first decade began at the age of 5.*

EXAMPLE (b): *26 days elapsed between the birthday and the start of the solar month. 26 divided by 3 = 8.66, so the first decade began at the age of 9.*

7 Completing the Life Cycle Decades You can now fill in the age at which each of the Life Cycle Decades begins, since the decades start at ten-year intervals. Thus, if the first decade began at the age of 5, the other decades would begin at ages 15, 25, 35, and so on. When you have done this, add the years corresponding to the beginning of each decade as an extra point of reference.

8 The Day Stem Element Finally, write the person's Day Stem Element (noted in Step 1) in the box marked 'Key Element'. This plays a central role in the interpretation of the Life Cycle Decades. With this last factor in place, the table is complete, and you are now ready to examine the significance of each decade of the person's life.

SETTING UP THE TABLE – AN EXAMPLE

To help you fill in your *Life Cycle Table*, this example shows how the table for Diana, Princess of Wales (see page 90), is compiled.

1 ▶ Name: *Diana, Princess of Wales* • Date of birth: *1 July 1961* • Sex (yang/yin): *female (yin)* • Birth Year (yang/yin): *yin* • Month Stem Element: *Yang Wood* • Month Animal Sign: *Horse* • Animal Element: *Yang Fire* • Day Stem Element: *Yin Wood*

2 ▶ Birth year = *yin* • Sex = *yin* • The polarity is the same, so the movement is forward.

3 ▶ The Natal Decade data is the same as that for the month of birth, thus the Natal Decade stem element is Yang Wood, the animal sign is Horse, and the animal element is Yang Fire. These are added to the table alongside 'Natal'.

4 ▶ The Cycle of Sixty chart shows that the Cyclical Number matching Yang Wood/Horse is 31. This is added to the table at the top of the No. column, alongside 'Natal'. In Step 2 we found that the movement is forward, so the No. column is completed with ascending Cyclical Numbers.

5 ▶ Using the Cycle of Sixty chart for reference, the factors for each decade are now added to the table next to each of the Cyclical Numbers.

6 ▶ The movement is forward, so Step 6a is used to work out the age corresponding to the beginning of each decade. Birthday = 1 July • Beginning of the next solar month = 7 July • Number of elapsed days = 6 • 6 divided by 3 = 2 • Thus 2 is the age at which the first decade begins.

7 ▶ The ages corresponding to the beginning of the decades can now be added; thus the first decade begins at 2, the second at 12, the third at 22, and so on. Once this is done, add the corresponding year next to each age.

8 ▶ Lastly, add the Day Stem Element (Yin Wood) in the 'Key Element' box. The table is now complete, and ready for interpretation.

INTERPRETING THE LIFE CYCLE TABLE

The interpretation of the horoscope and the Life Cycle Table requires a certain amount of intuitive inspiration. This will become easier once you are more familiar with the relationships between the various factors involved. These guidelines will help you assemble the factors needed to discover the more fruitful and less favourable periods in a person's life.

The Key Factor

Unlike the horoscope chart, the key factor in the Life Cycle Decades is not the animal sign for the year, but the stem element for the day. This is the Key Element. Each decade of the Life Cycle Table has two elements. Compare these with the Key Element to see whether they affect it favourably or unfavourably. For a quick-reference guide, turn to the table on the opening page for each element section (pages 74–83). For an in-depth reminder, see Sequences of the Elements on page 17.

• *Remember: Key Element = stem element for day of birth*

Yang or Yin Elements

It is important to take into account whether the elements are yang or yin – their effects are different. For example, suppose the Key Element is Yang Wood, and that the two elements for a particular decade are Yang Water (stem element) and Yang Metal (animal element), while those for the following decade are Yin Water and Yin Metal. The table of important factors on page 75 reveals that Yang Metal is harmful to Yang Wood, whereas Yin Metal is beneficial. Thus the second of the two decades would be more favourable than the first.

• *Remember: Note whether the elements are yang or yin*

• *Hint: The two elements for a decade will have the same polarity (they cannot be a mixture of yin and yang)*

The Earlier and Later Five-Yearly Periods

The stem element and the animal sign element of the decade are taken together when considering the effect they are likely to have on the progress of a person's life. But, as a general rule, the stem element has greater influence during the first five years of a decade, while the animal sign element is more influential during the latter five years.

Comparing the Influencing Elements

The two elements found in each decade are known as the Influencing Elements – both of these are compared in turn with the Key Element. But they should also be compared with each other. If one of the two Influencing Elements is harmful, its unfavourable effect may be neutralized by the other.

• *Remember: Compare the two Influencing Elements both separately and combined together*

Comparing the Animal Sign with Different Years

You can also compare the animal sign of a decade with that for each of the years in the decade, to see which are most favourable. For example, suppose the decade was from 1988 to 1997 inclusive, and that the animal sign for that decade was the Rabbit. The effects of that decade, as revealed by the Influencing Elements, would thus be at their peak during years harmonious with the Rabbit: 1987 (Rabbit), 1991 (Sheep) and 1995 (Pig). Conversely, during 1993 (Rooster) the effect would be weaker.

• *Remember: Use the decade animal to find out when the effects of the Influencing Elements are at their strongest and weakest*

PUTTING
IT
ALL

TOGETHER

The previous sections have explained the fundamentals on which Chinese astrology is based. Now here is a reminder of those topics which help unravel the mysteries of the Chinese horoscope chart. The following pointers will direct you through the several stages of compiling a horoscope chart and Life Cycle Table, and – just as importantly – how to interpret what the ancient sages referred to as the 'Revelations of the Celestial Messengers'. Record the details of each chart you create using a copy of the blank horoscope grid on page 16 of the chart booklet. This not only allows you to re-use the cards for future charts, but also enables you to compare charts that you have already compiled.

First you need to assemble the horoscope chart. Make a note of the person's date and time of birth. Following the instructions on pages 24–5, choose the eight horoscope cards which represent the stem and branch of the year, month, day and hour of birth. Place the seven-sided card representing the person's birth year in the centre of the horoscope chart, and the remaining seven cards around it. You can now begin to interpret your chart (*see step-by-step guide, right*).

To guide you through the mysteries of horoscope interpretation, the analyses of two different horoscopes are included on the following pages – those of Diana, Princess of Wales, and Albert Einstein, whose lives perhaps could not have been in greater contrast.

What to do

1 Initial interpretation First, compare the animal sign in the centre with the three other animal signs in the chart. A useful method is to visualize the twelve animal signs arranged round a clock-face. Those signs which are four 'hours' apart – for example, the Rat, Dragon and Monkey – are favourable combinations, but those which are three or six hours apart, such as the Rat, Rabbit and Horse, are unfavourable combinations. Further information is given in the relevant section on each animal sign.

PIG · RAT · OX · DOG · TIGER · ROOSTER · RABBIT · MONKEY · DRAGON · SHEEP · SNAKE · HORSE

—— FAVOURABLE
- - - UNFAVOURABLE

2 The inner character The central card gives a rough overview of the outward personality of someone belonging to that particular sign. By comparing the central animal card with the other three animal cards in the horoscope chart, you can develop a more in-depth assessment of the person's inner character. You can also compare the central card with that of another person's horoscope chart to assess the compatibility between the two signs (you can find more detailed information on compatibility in each of the animal sections).

3 What lies ahead in the coming year Still focusing on the central animal card, you can also make a general assessment of the coming year's potential by comparing the animal sign of the coming year with that of the central card of the horoscope (again, you will need to refer to the compatibility between the two signs).

4 Weighing the five elements Once you have assessed the animal signs in the chart, you can move on to the elements. Make a note of the number of cards for each element, and whether the elements are yang or yin. The element 'weightings' (irrespective of whether they are yang or yin) are used to evaluate potential creativity, authority, tenacity, ambition and communication. Turn to the sample horoscope readings on the following pages for examples of how to record the elemental weighting.

5 Comparing the Key Element with the other elements The Key Element is the stem element for the day of birth. This is the card that sits at the top of the horoscope chart (card position 6). When comparing the Key Element with the other elements in the chart, remember that the effect of the elements often depends on whether they are yang or yin. Again, you may find it helpful to draw up a table like the one shown to the right, detailing the Key Element and the other elements in the chart. It is also useful to note whether each element supports, or is supported by, the Key Element.

6 Searching for vital elements Once you know which elements are supportive, and which are not, you can use this information when examining the Life Cycle Table. For example, we know that the Key Element for Diana, Princess of Wales, is Yin Wood. From the Wood table on page 75, we see that the element which supports it, bringing happiness, is Water. Sadly this is missing from the horoscope. Wealth, however, there is in plenty.

7 Some additional hints When you look at the animal signs, see if they are in balance or not. Look for special groups or patterns, such as the Four Triangles or the Three Crosses (*see page 15*). Note which of the four 'houses' they occupy (Creativity, Development, Spirituality, Sexuality, Career or Home Life). If any oppose each other, make a note of the house which appears to be under threat from an opposing sign, and check if the threatened sign is supported by a 'friendly animal'. For example, if the Rooster in the Career house is under threat from the Rabbit, judge whether it is supported or weakened by other animal signs in the horoscope chart.

8 Links to the Key Element While it is, of course, fundamental to assess the balance of the elements in the chart, don't forget that the polarity of the elements affects their relationship with the Key Element. Look out for the special links to the Key Element: the Unexpected Wealth and the Earned Wealth; the Happiness; the Unfavourable Sign (significantly known to Chinese astrologers as the 'Seventh Curse'); and the Beneficial Change. These are all detailed in the table of important factors at the end of each separate element section.

9 The ancient stem signs Don't forget, also, the historical background to the ten stem signs. It is always worth referring back to the introductory paragraphs on each of the five elements to see if some special meaning might be gleaned from the ancient signs. For instance, stem 1 (Yang Wood), representing a baby, may have some special significance in a person's horoscope. And stem 10 (Yin Water) definitely has a mystical implication which lies outside its element significance. In addition, stems which follow in sequence usually show career or society advancement. In particular, stems 1, 2 and 3 (Yang Wood, Yin Wood and Yang Fire) show a rise to a position of power.

KEY ELEMENT: *Yin Wood*

WOOD	
Yang	Yin
1	2
pair *good*	match *neutral*

FIRE	
Yang	Yin
1	–
child *supported*	child *supported*

EARTH	
Yang	Yin
–	3
destroyed *poor*	destroyed *poor*

METAL	
Yang	Yin
–	1
destroys *poor*	destroys *poor*

WATER	
Yang	Yin
–	–
parent *supports*	parent *supports*

SAMPLE READING ONE

NAME: Diana, Princess of Wales
DATE OF BIRTH: 1 July 1961
TIME OF BIRTH: 06:45
MARRIED: 29 July 1981
DIVORCED: 28 August 1996
DIED: 30 August 1997

The Second Column (*month*)
ANIMAL: Horse (Yang Fire)
ELEMENT: Yang Wood

The Third Column (*day*)
ANIMAL: Sheep (Yin Earth)
KEY ELEMENT: Yin Wood

The Fourth Column (*hour*)
ANIMAL: Rabbit (Yin Wood)
ELEMENT: Yin Earth

The First Column (*year*)
ANIMAL: Ox (Yin Earth)
ELEMENT: Yin Metal

DECADE	YEAR	AGE	NO.	STEM ELEMENT	ANIMAL SIGN	ANIMAL ELEMENT	SIGNIFICANT YEARS	ANIMAL SIGN OF YEAR
Natal	1961	–	31	*Yang Wood*	*Horse*	*Yang Fire*	1961	*Ox*
1ST	1963	2	32	*Yin Wood*	*Sheep*	*Yin Earth*	–	–
2ND	1973	12	33	*Yang Fire*	*Monkey*	*Yang Metal*	1981 *Marriage*	*Rooster*
3RD	1983	22	34	*Yin Fire*	*Rooster*	*Yin Metal*	1992 *Separation*	*Monkey*
4TH	1993	32	35	*Yang Earth*	*Dog*	*Yang Earth*	1996 *Divorce* / 1997 *Death*	*Rat* / *Ox*

THE ANIMAL SIGNS

Diana, Princess of Wales, was born in 1961, the year of the Ox. This factor gave Diana the essential seeds of determination and stubbornness which were to be such a notable feature of her private life.

The other animal signs in her chart include the Rabbit and Sheep, the former revealing her caring attitude as the source of the inspiration for her work with the deprived and underprivileged. This aspect was given stronger impetus by the Sheep, which supports and harmonizes with the Rabbit. The Sheep itself is often a sign of musical talent, and although Diana did not become a professional musician, she once demonstrated her remarkable artistic talents playing the piano in public, and on one celebrated occasion, made a surprise appearance on stage as a dancer, to the delight of everyone except her husband, Prince Charles.

Her marriage to Charles ought to have been happy: he was born in the year of the Rat, and she in the Ox, and both are the yang and yin sides of the first house – Creativity. Yet her fourth animal, the Horse, stands defiantly against the Rat, while within her own chart the Ox strikes directly opposite the partnership of the Sheep and the Horse.

1981 was significant for Diana – the year of the Rooster, one of the best signs for the Ox. Diana was then at the peak of her happiness, as she married the Prince in fairytale style. However, 1992, the year of the Monkey, was the year in which the couple separated. 'There are signs that matters are going to go your way', reveals the text for Ox fortunes in a Monkey year. For Diana, this meant the shackles of marriage being thrown off. In 1996, a Rat year favourable to Charles, they divorced. It was during an Ox year that Diana met her tragic death. As the text for Ox people in Ox years states: 'Matters may come to a halt during the year of the Ox.' For Diana, it was a full stop.

THE STEMS AND ELEMENTS

Diana's horoscope nearly includes the 'royal' sequence of stems 1, 2 and 3. Yang Wood for her month stem element and Yin Wood for her day stem element (her Key Element, together with its yang counterpart, ensuring success) are the first two stems, but the third, Yang Fire, belongs to the animal sign of her month. She was on the way to becoming queen, but never completed the journey.

Her Key Element of Yin Wood underlines the role she played helping underprivileged children. The fact that there is no supporting Water in the chart suggests that her childhood was not entirely happy, lacking parental comfort. But the 'child' of Wood, Fire, is present, showing that she was not slow to offer her own children the love that had been missing from her own childhood.

Yet Yin Earth is very strong, indicating Unexpected Wealth. She was a hard worker, but it must also be stressed that her popularity, influence and privilege were gained through marriage.

THE LIFE CYCLE DECADES

For Yin Wood, Yang Metal is the sign of Beneficial Change. This appears in her horoscope as an auspicious sign, but is the ruling element in the latter part of the second decade, when she married – a dramatic beneficial change. But when Metal turned from yang to yin, in the last year of the third decade, she and Charles separated.

But the effect of the Yin Metal had only just begun. The attack on her Key Element saw her decline – and ultimate fall. She offended many of her supporters when she withdrew her patronage of several of the charities which she had backed, and in the remaining years of her short life recklessly involved herself with a string of admirers, whose careers and lives were ruined as a result.

The fourth decade was disastrous. The double Earth, which had brought her riches, was now too heavy, and toppled her. First came the final divorce, and then – almost a year to the day later – she met her fateful end. Yang Water, which would have been the symbol of happiness for Diana, is missing from her horoscope chart. Had she lived until she was 42, her next Life Cycle Decade would have brought the Water – and the happiness – that seems to have eluded her in life.

WOOD	
Yang	Yin
1	2
FIRE	
Yang	Yin
1	–
EARTH	
Yang	Yin
–	3
METAL	
Yang	Yin
–	1
WATER	
Yang	Yin
–	–

NAME: Albert Einstein
DATE OF BIRTH: 14 March 1879
TIME OF BIRTH: 11:30
MARRIED: 1903, 1919
DIED: 18 April 1955

The Third Column (*day*)
ANIMAL: Monkey (Yang Metal)
KEY ELEMENT: Yang Fire

The Fourth Column (*hour*)
ANIMAL: Horse (Yang Fire)
ELEMENT: Yang Wood

The Second Column (*month*)
ANIMAL: Rabbit (Yin Wood)
ELEMENT: Yin Fire

The First Column (*year*)
ANIMAL: Rabbit (Yin Wood)
ELEMENT: Yin Earth

DECADE	YEAR	AGE	NO.	STEM ELEMENT	ANIMAL SIGN	ANIMAL ELEMENT
Natal	1879	–	4	Yin Fire	Rabbit	Yin Wood
1ST	1882	3	3	Yang Fire	Tiger	Yang Wood
2ND	1892	13	2	Yin Wood	Ox	Yin Earth
3RD	1902	23	1	Yang Wood	Rat	Yang Water
4TH	1912	33	60	Yin Water	Pig	Yin Water
5TH	1922	43	59	Yang Water	Dog	Yang Earth
6TH	1932	53	58	Yin Metal	Rooster	Yin Metal
7TH	1942	63	57	Yang Metal	Monkey	Yang Metal
8TH	1952	73	56	Yin Earth	Sheep	Yin Earth

Albert Einstein

Lightning had been flashing through the skies aeons before electricity had been harnessed by the human race. But 2 December 1942 was a critical moment in the history of the earth, for it was on that date that the first nuclear reaction was artificially created outside the fierce furnaces of the very stars themselves. It was an event conceived some forty years earlier – and seen through to its dreadful conclusion as the atomic bomb – by the man described as the greatest intellectual genius of the age: Albert Einstein.

NOTE: *As Einstein's date of birth is earlier than the commencement of the tables included in this pack, the necessary data has been accessed from original Chinese calendars.*

92

THE ANIMAL SIGNS

Einstein was born in a Rabbit year – indeed, there are two Rabbits in Einstein's horoscope chart. It might be thought that a person of such stature would have been born in a year designated by a more charismatic animal – a Tiger or Dragon perhaps. But the Rabbits reveal Einstein as an active pacifist – he founded the Einstein War Resister's International Fund, abhorred war, and spent much of his life trying to bring harmony to the world. The tragic irony was that his belief had to be turned on its head: in 1933, fearful of the way matters were progressing in Europe, he had no other course but to advise President Roosevelt that America build an atomic bomb before anyone else did, and he was active in its construction. This culminated in 1945, a Rooster year – a sign directly opposed to the Rabbit. It was also a Rooster year (1933) when Einstein broke with his past, left Germany and moved to America for good.

The Horse, conflicting with the two Rabbits (the two signs are three 'hours' apart), reveals Einstein's inner angst – trying to reconcile his desire to bring peace to the world with the fact that he was the architect of its weapons of mass destruction. It was in a Horse year, 1942, that the first artificial nuclear chain reaction was effected. The Monkey in Einstein's chart occupies the House of Career, and marks the source of his technological skill.

He married twice – the first time in 1903, a Rabbit year. But although it was a happy marriage, the First World War obliged the couple to separate; his wife was unable to return to Germany, and they divorced. But happiness returned in 1919, a Sheep year (favourable to the Rabbit), when he married a second time. It was also in the harmonious Sheep year that his theories were proved correct, through an ingenious experiment carried out during the total eclipse of the Sun.

THE STEMS AND ELEMENTS

The element pairings in the chart are remarkable. The stems 1, 2 and 3 show Einstein to be a top achiever. His Key Element, Yang Fire, is matched with its counterpart, Yin Fire, ensuring success. The strong support of the creative 'parent' Wood element is borne out by the fact that his love of science and mathematics was instilled by his parents.

Water is missing from the horoscope, but unlike in Diana's case, where Water signified happiness, the absence is not as critical. In fact, there is a strong presence of happiness in Einstein's chart, as it is signified by Yin Wood.

THE LIFE CYCLE DECADES

The elements for the Natal Decade and the first two decades perfectly match the elements in Einstein's horoscope: Yin Fire and Yin Wood, Yang Fire and Yang Wood, and Yin Wood and Yin Earth. This was a strongly formative period during which the young Einstein decided that his ambition in life was to solve the riddle of the universe – the 'unifying theory'. In later decades, after Einstein had published his famous equation, and been awarded the Nobel prize for an entirely different theory, his Life Cycle Decades take on a curious quality: stem and branch remain paired – unified, one might say – for each decade up until the end of his life.

WOOD	
Yang	Yin
1	2
FIRE	
Yang	Yin
2	1
EARTH	
Yang	Yin
–	1
METAL	
Yang	Yin
1	–
WATER	
Yang	Yin
–	–

DAYS FOR

CUTTING CLOTHES

Most Chinese calendars and diaries indicate suitable days for all kinds of activities, both personal and business. They are known as 'Clothes-Cutting Days' because in the ancient text which first described them, the first two words were 'Cut Clothes'. Originally, their intended purpose was to make the Chinese calendar more accurate, but their association with everyday affairs became entrenched in Chinese social life (when a nineteenth-century emperor decided to abolish them, it nearly caused a revolution – it was feared that if people did not know what to do on certain days, the empire would be thrown into chaos). They are still used today, but not taken so literally.

Find out how to consult the Clothes-Cutting Days below, to discover the most suitable days for a whole range of activities.

How to use the wheel

1 Turn to the back flap of the chart booklet, cut out the two dials and follow the simple instructions on how to assemble your Clothes-Cutting Days wheel.

2 Once your wheel is assembled, look up the animal sign for the required day by consulting charts 3 and 4 in the booklet (pages 9 – 11). For example, if the day in question is 22 October 2001, you would discover that this is a Horse day.

3 Turn the inner dial of your wheel so that the animal sign of the day (Horse, in our example) is lined up with the Chinese solar month that contains the day in question (in this case 8 Oct – 6 Nov). The month dates are printed around the outside of the dial forming the base of the wheel.

4 Note the letter shown through the window on the inner dial (remember that the window is in the segment relating to your Year Animal). Then refer to the lists of *Beneficial Activities* and *Things to Avoid Doing* to discover the favourable and unfavourable activities for that day. For example, if you were born in the year of the Dog, this gives you the letter **K** for 22 October 2001; beneficial activities include crafts, making things, weddings and travel, while arranging funerals for that day should be avoided.

The wheel shown opposite has been set up according to the example used in Steps 1 to 4 (Horse Day – 22 October 2001, for someone born in a Dog year). To use the wheel for more than one person you will need to cut out all the windows, since the letter denoting a person's fortune is the one that appears underneath their Year Animal.

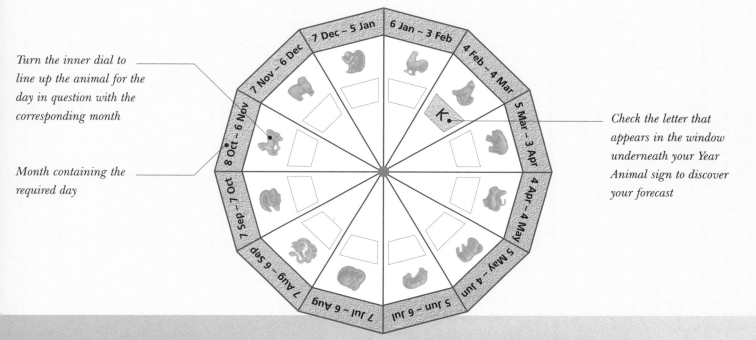

Turn the inner dial to line up the animal for the day in question with the corresponding month

Month containing the required day

Check the letter that appears in the window underneath your Year Animal sign to discover your forecast

Wheel labels (clockwise from top): 6 Jan – 3 Feb, 4 Feb – 4 Mar, 5 Mar – 3 Apr, 4 Apr – 4 May, 5 May – 4 Jun, 5 Jun – 6 Jul, 7 Jul – 6 Aug, 7 Aug – 6 Sep, 7 Sep – 7 Oct, 8 Oct – 6 Nov, 7 Nov – 6 Dec, 7 Dec – 5 Jan

BENEFICIAL ACTIVITIES

- A *Cut clothes, trade, do accounts, travel on land*
- B *Clean, sweep, wash, bathe, swim*
- C *Weddings, moving house, journeys*
- D *Weddings, moving house, decorating, meditation*
- E *Gardening, cleaning drains, diverting streams, weddings*
- F *Gardening, cleaning drains, diverting streams, weddings*
- G *Go fishing!*
- H *Drink wine and enjoy yourself!*
- I *Favourable for most activities*
- J *Use savings, carry on trade, get engaged, arrange weddings*
- K *Crafts, making things, weddings, travel*
- L *Put up notices, advertise, write letters, read uplifting books*

THINGS TO AVOID DOING

- A *Digging, travel on water, drawing out savings*
- B *Weddings, travel, digging wells*
- C *Gardening, dealing with water supplies*
- D *Gardening, dealing with water supplies*
- E *Making accusations or voicing suspicions*
- F *Moving house, travel, drawing on savings*
- G *Work*
- H *Business deals and commerce*
- I *Saying unpleasant things about people*
- J *Funerals, travel or acupuncture*
- K *Arranging funerals for this day*
- L *Entertaining business clients*

FURTHER READING

Chinese Almanacs, Richard Smith. Hong Kong: Oxford University Press, 1992.

Chinese Creeds and Customs, V. R. Burkhardt. Hong Kong: South China Morning Post, 1953.

Chinese Customs, Henry Doré (reprint of 'Researches into Chinese Superstitions' Part 1, Vol I, 1911). Singapore: Graham Brash, 1987.

Doctors, Diviners, and Magicians of Ancient China, Kenneth J. DeWoskin. New York: Columbia University Press, 1983.

Chinese Horoscopes, Paula Delsol. London: Pan Books, 1973.

Chinese Zodiac Signs, Catherine Aubier and Josanne Delangre (trans. Eileen Finletter and Ian Murray). London: Treasure Press, 1998.

The Way to Chinese Astrology, Jean-Michel Huon de Kermadec and N. Derek Poulsen. London: Unwin, 1983.

Other titles of interest by Derek Walters:

Chinese Astrology: Interpreting the Revelations of the Celestial Messengers. London: Aquarian Press, 1987.

Chinese Love Signs. Torrance, CA: Heian, 1997.

Ming Shu: The Art and Practice of Chinese Astrology. New York: Simon and Schuster, 1987.

ABOUT THE AUTHOR

DEREK WALTERS was born in Manchester, England, in the year of the Fire Rat. He is an internationally renowned authority on Chinese astrology and feng shui. One of the pioneers of feng shui in the Western hemisphere (the celebrated author Lillian Too affectionately dubbed him the 'Grandfather' of Western feng shui) he is also respected for his academic knowledge, his book on the history of Chinese astrology – *Chinese Astrology: Interpreting the Revelations of the Celestial Messengers* – being the standard work on the subject. Other books on Chinese Traditional Culture, including the popular *Feng Shui Handbook,* have been translated into more than twenty languages, including Japanese. Though now resident in the northern seaside town of Morecambe, England, he still makes frequent visits to the Far East and is a member of the Scientific Organising Committee for the international symposia on Chinese Astronomy and Traditional Culture at the Purple Mountain University, Academia Sinica, Nanjing, as well as being an honorary member of the Society of Diviners, Hong Kong.

While officially retired, he nevertheless still lectures regularly in Germany, and has recently inaugurated courses in Russia and the countries of the former Soviet Union.

ABOUT THE ARTIST

HELEN JONES is an illustrator whose work has been highly acclaimed both in the US and the UK. Here, she has taken the complex subject of Chinese astrology and – with Derek Walters' expert advice – devised this exciting set of horoscope cards to help make compiling a horoscope an easier and, hopefully, more entertaining task.

Helen's distinctive three-dimensional style is published in books, magazines and newspapers across Europe and the US, and includes a complete tarot deck in the form of *The Renaissance Tarot* (by Jane Lyle), which has been published worldwide. Her work also finds diverse applications ranging from CD covers to murals for shop interiors.

ACKNOWLEDGEMENTS

Helen Jones would like to thank Nick for his support and enthusiasm for the project from the beginning; Tessa, for the heroic task of editing such a complicated book; Pritty and Braz, for work above and beyond the call of duty on the beautiful charts; and, last but not least, Derek, for his teaching on the subject of all things Chinese.

EDDISON ◆ SADD EDITIONS

Editorial Director	Ian Jackson
Senior Editor	Tessa Monina
Editor	Nicola Hodgson
Proofreader	Nikky Twyman
Creative Director	Nick Eddison
Art Director	Elaine Partington
Senior Art Editor	Pritty Ramjee
Mac Designer	Brazzle Atkins
Card Photography	Stephen Marwood
Image Manipulation	Anthony Duke
Production	Karyn Claridge and Charles James